Published by Innovative Grammar

Copyright ©2010 by Janelle Cameron and Kevin Clark

Cover design by Joel D. Castro

Lightning Source edition: October 2011

ISBN: 978-0-9838990-0-6

About the Authors

Innovative Grammar is a consortium of ELD teachers and researchers who exchange ideas, knowledge and effective practices in the teaching of English grammar, both to English learners and to English-only students.

Janelle Cameron is a language development and literacy consultant from Sacramento, CA. She works nationally with teachers in grades K-12.

Kevin Clark is president of Clark Consulting and Training, Inc., a national organization specializing in the design, implementation and measurement of language development programs for English learners and English-only students. His company is located in Clovis, CA.

—

ABOUT THIS GUIDE

This guide is designed to accomplish three specific goals for teachers:

- Minimize teacher preparation time
- Provide a consistent format for grammar lessons
- Utilize similar terminology and student samples

Included in this book are all of the pre-prepared charts needed for teaching verb tenses and grammar to English learners (and non-English learners) of all ability levels and age ranges. The tools included here cover the simplest aspects of English grammar to advanced concepts and applications for students approaching English mastery. The order of the charts is also consistent with how most states and districts organize grammar concepts, starting with foundational elements and moving hierarchically to more advanced elements.

This guide is laid out in a very user-friendly format. The first section provides a brief description of the language star, which answers the question: *What is ELD*? From there, clear and concise definitions for each part of speech are included. In this section is also a description of something called the *Grammar Wall*, which is essentially a physical space in your room that is used for organizing the various parts of speech you have taught. Its uses are many, and it is equally effective with novice language learners as with those approaching full English competence.

The bulk of the guide follows, with preview charts organized in two easy-to-use ways.

Getting Started: This section features all the charts and concepts you need to begin ELD instruction for students new to the language, or those who could benefit from a review of the fundamentals. This section is marked by a tab at the top of each page.

Basic: This section is a collection of the charts and language skills that correspond to students who have language skills up to an intermediate competence level. This section is marked by a tab at the mid-point of each page.

Advanced: This portion of the guide is for students who are ready to tackle the more complex elements of language, or for students who "seem" to speak English fluently but who lack a solid grammatical understanding and control of the language. This section corresponds to the table lowest on the pages.

The second organization system utilized in this guide is by part of speech. Using the index at the front of the guide, you simply locate the part of speech you want to teach, and then find more specific concepts listed underneath. The page number is noted and off you go.

Early in the guide is a list of common questions asked by teachers and administrators about grammar and language teaching. The answers are designed to save you time and energy, as well as to provide some field-tested advice and insights from years of practice.

In short, what you have here is an all-inclusive toolbox for making your English grammar teaching more efficient, effective and rewarding for both you and your students.

Table of Contents

Looking for Something Specific?

What is English Language Development?

Probably the most common question asked by teachers who are assigned to ELD instruction is: What is ELD? Though on the surface the question seems simple, there are many possible answers. We will rely here on a definition of language that breaks it down into its basic parts, or elements. In a grammar-based language program, this definition helps to organize teaching, since we can identify the aspect of language students need and then teach them an appropriate skill from that particular domain.

There are five aspects of English—or any language, for that matter-- that are important to understand. By seeing how each works in conjunction with the others, teachers can better understand how to design, develop and execute lessons that focus on particular elements of the language. This also helps teachers to better select appropriate methods to use. For this discussion, it is helpful to think of language as a five-pointed star. On each spire of the star is a particular element, or aspect, of language.

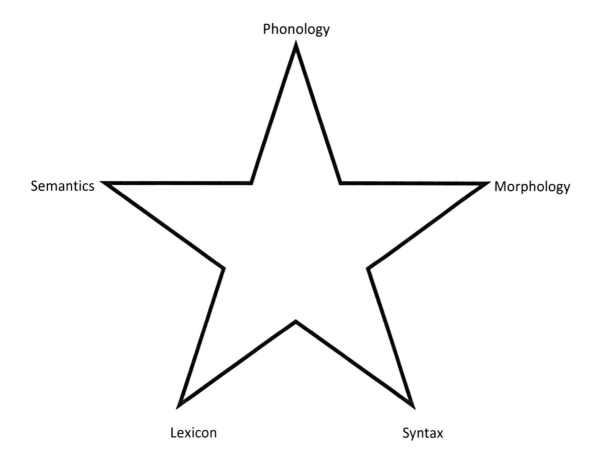

Let's take a quick look at each of these.

Phonology: This aspect of language is concerned with the smallest units of sound in a language. English has approximately 44 different sounds that are combined to form the words in the language. By contrast, the Spanish language has only 24 sounds, or phonemes. On a practical level, phonology refers to a student's ability to actually produce and hear each of these individual sounds. The importance of phonological development for English learners is vital. Without being able to hear the sounds, or produce those sounds, it is difficult for students to understand phonics. Spelling correctly is also highly dependent on phonology. It is frequently assumed that students will develop an "ear" for language without direct instruction. Unfortunately, this does not seem to be the case, and most English learners require consistent, explicit and guided instruction in how to hear and produce the sounds of the English language.

Morphology: This is the study of the smallest units of meaningful sound in a language. This sounds complex, but it's actually pretty simple. In other words, it is about the prefixes and suffixes-- and other word "affixes"-- that can change the meaning of a word. For example, take the word "cat." How many separate "meaningful" sounds are there? Well, first there is the word itself, *cat*. Then there is the word *at*. So there are two morphemes in the word *cat*. What if we add an "s" to the word, making it *cats*? Now there are three morphemes, since the addition of the sound /s/ is meaningful, signifying more than one cat. Another important element of morphology is the range of word endings used in English to represent verb tenses. By adding "ed", "ing" or "s" to a root verb, we can change the meaning that is being conveyed. For example, the meaning of "walk" is changed substantially when we add these endings: *walked, walking, walks*. A big piece of grammar teaching is consumed by verb tense instruction. A simple review of writing produced by English learners usually reveals a poor understanding of how to construct and apply the English verb tense system. Pre-prepared charts are included in this book for all of the English language verb tenses, and their related formulas.

Syntax: This refers to the rules that govern the order of words in a language. English, like other languages, relies on its own set of syntax rules. For instance, adjectives frequently come before nouns, as in: *The red car*. Articles always precede nouns, as in: *A red car*. Verbs tend to follow the subject of a sentence, while prepositions come before nouns. There are others, but the important thing to understand is that without these word order rules, students' English writing can suffer badly, as can their reading comprehension. A solid understanding of syntax also is essential for learning, using and retaining new vocabulary. The direct teaching of English syntax is one of the most neglected elements of English language teaching in classrooms. You have probably already seen in the table of contents the range of pre-prepared tools in this book for teaching these useful—and sometimes even exciting --rules of English word order.

Lexicon: In technical terms, lexicon refers to the total stock of morphemes in a language. More simply, lexicon is the supply of words available to a person. For example, there is a lexicon of golf, which includes an entire word bank of phrases, nouns and verbs that only make sense to other golfers. Likewise, teachers typically share a specialized lexicon; words that are meaningful to them in the context of teaching, but may be incomprehensible to non-educators. Many English learners have sizeable lexicons; they know a lot of words. Unfortunately, what is frequently lacking is the knowledge of how to use those words in sentences and with the proper meanings. It is not uncommon to see English learners writing -- and even memorizing-- long lists of words for which they do not know the meanings, nor how to use them skillfully in real sentences. You can probably see how the previous discussion of syntax links to this element of language.

Semantics: This is the study of word meanings. Together with lexicon, we could refer to these as vocabulary-- knowing a word, its meaning and how to use it in a sentence properly. The English language can be a semantic minefield for English learners since so many words have multiple meanings that often depend on where and how they are used in a sentence. It frequently seems that just when we have taught our students what a word means, that word pops up in another sentence or context where it means something completely different. That is the wonderful – and sometimes frustrating—world of semantics. Still, semantics can be seen by students as a fun exploration of the English language. The *Grammar Wall* can be a rich teaching tool to help students to see how vocabulary functions and changes within the context of the English grammar system.

Together, these fundamental aspects form the internal components of the large system we call language. By having a working knowledge of these components, teachers can better understand how to plan and deliver instruction that focuses on one or more of these elements. Certainly, some of these areas will develop more rapidly than others, though each English learner typically presents a unique profile of development. By using the language star as a guide, we can also make sure that we are not tilting our instruction too heavily in only one or two areas. For students to be considered balanced and proficient English users, they must have high levels of competence in all areas. The resources in this book are designed to accomplish just that.

Q & A: The Top 10 Grammar-Teaching Questions

1. Q: *Is it enough to just copy the charts from this book and begin using them?*

    A: If you are a skilled ELD practitioner, the charts may be all you need to supplement your own knowledge and experience with the grammar concept. For others, the charts should help to narrow your own learning objective. Sometimes, the preview chart, together with the definitions of the relevant part of speech, is enough to jog the grammar memory of teachers who may have studied the grammar concept at some earlier time. In some cases, the charts included here can supplement additional resources you may consult to better understand a certain grammar concept.

2. Q: *Should students be provided their own copies of the various preview charts from this book?*

    A: Some teachers, particularly of older students (grades four and above), have found that students benefit tremendously from having their own grammar resources, including the preview charts in this book. Secondary age students, in particular, have used the charts productively as study aids and notes organizers.

3. Q: *Do the preview charts here have to be larger for students to be able to see them?*

    A: Usually, teachers copy the information from the preview charts in this book onto larger chart-size paper, or blow them up though the use of a document camera or other magnifying device. In either case, it is obviously important that all students involved in the lesson be able to see the ideas, definitions and graphics provided on the preview charts. Writing on the charts with bold marking pen colors boosts clarity considerably, and the use of one or two colors of ink can help to emphasize different aspects of the chart. There is no need to use every color of the rainbow. The value of a hand-written chart—versus one produced electronically—is cited again and again by teachers as a major factor in converting the paper from just a "chart" into an enduring and useful grammar-teaching tool that students look to as a resource.

4. Q: *Can these charts be used with electronic projection systems?*

    A: Some very skilled teachers have used their charts effectively on Promethean boards and other types of electronic instructional tools. It should be noted, however, that this type of usage does not allow for developing a physical inventory of language resources that students and teachers can refer to in the course of other lessons.

5. Q: *Do I have to use only the sample sentences already provided on the charts?*

    A: The sentences on the preview charts are designed to closely follow the grammar concept, verb tense or other concept under study. This allows teachers to spend more time teaching than preparing. However, additional sentences can certainly be added if they support students' learning and understanding. The use of sentences that are specifically designed for a particular grade level or language proficiency level is certainly helpful. Also, consider including in the sentences ideas, concepts or events that relate to what students already know or are studying. Sometimes, including relevant content from science or other subject areas boosts the impact of the sentences and helps to better show the importance of the grammar concept under study.

6. Q: *Can I make copies of the charts in the book for other teachers?*

    A: Each of the charts in this book, along with the other instructional resources, is copyrighted and is for the sole use of the purchaser of the book.

7. Q: *Where can I find more information on grammar concepts that I need to review myself?*

    A: A good source for reviewing grammar concepts is *Checking Your Grammar: And Getting it Right* available from Scholastic publishers. There are other quality resources available on the Internet.

8. Q: *Can I use the charts in the book out of order?*

    A: Yes. While the charts in the book follow a commonly accepted order of grammar skill teaching for English learners, that does not mean they can't be used in an order that better suits the linguistic needs of students.

9. Q: *Should I use the actual terminology on the charts, even for younger students?*

    A: Much like we teach young student mathematics with the same nomenclature as for older students, the same is true for grammar teaching. The use of a common lexicon for grammar teaching actually helps students to better understand the components of grammar. We have seen students in pre-kindergarten classes have passionate discussions about adjectives, pronouns and the relative utility of the present progressive tense.

10. Q: *For how long should I use a particular preview chart?*

    A: This might depend on your local or state pacing guide for grammar instruction. However, since so many grammar concepts build on a prior skill, it seems logical to ensure that students have a good understanding and ability to use a particular skill before moving on to more difficult concepts. Periodic reviews of foundational grammar ideas can also prove helpful before venturing into new territory.

Getting Started

Resources

- *Grammar Wall* Description
- *Grammar Wall* Template
- Parts of Speech Definitions
- Parts of Speech Table
- *Grammar Study* Description
- Verb Tense Table
- Verb Tense Timeline
- *Verb Tense Study* Description
- Blank Preview Chart

Concept Charts

- Types of Sentences
- Singular and Plural Nouns
- Types of Verbs
- Pronouns and To be Verbs

Description

The *Grammar Wall* is a large wall area dedicated to displaying categorized words that belong to each of the eight parts of speech.

Purpose

The *Grammar Wall* serves three important purposes in a language-teaching program. First, it functions as a three-dimensional grammar book, where words are slotted into categories with clear written explanations. Second, the *Grammar Wall* is an on-going instructional tool since it is the central repository for all words that have been analyzed in the *Syntax Surgery* method. Third, it serves students and teachers as a living thesaurus as they work with other grammar concepts and with other grammar-teaching instructional methods. By having an at-the-ready visual thesaurus, students can both learn new concepts as well as revisit prior concepts.

Key Language Skills

All eight parts of speech.

Materials

You will need colored paper placards that identify each part of speech and provide a clear definition. Ideally, you want a wall surface that is approximately 12 feet wide and at least four feet high. You can use three-by-five, or slightly smaller, cards to write new words on and affix them to the grammar wall with push pins or tape. A bright-colored yarn can be useful to connect items on advanced grammar walls that have subcategories within the part of speech. For example, verbs might have the following sub-categories: action, mental, state of being, transitive, intransitive.

Procedure

Step 1: Start by crafting the placards for each part of speech. Use the definitions included in this book. Write them clearly in marker using colors that are easily visible from a distance. Place them across the top of your *Grammar Wall* approximately 18 inches apart in the order shown on the diagram in this section of the guide.

Step 2: Add words to each category by taping or pinning them in the appropriate category. Of course, the discussions you have with students are by far the most important part. The actual pinning of the word represents the final aspect of this process.

Step 3: As new concepts are taught and explored, add them as sub-categories to your *Grammar Wall*. Place them under the larger category heading (verb, nouns, pronouns, etc.). For example, proper nouns or abstract nouns might be added to the noun category. Consider using yarn to show a linear relationship between the major category and the sub-categories.

Hot Tips

1. Be careful with the capital letters. Erratic use of capitals can confuse students when you put the words on the wall.
2. Make all verbs infinitive. If you want to put the verb "walk" on the wall, convert it to its base for: to walk. This avoids confusing it with other possible parts of speech (walk = noun).
3. Make it a regular part of your grammar instruction. Consider adding words immediately after completing a *Syntax Surgery* while the words and the grammar concept under study are fresh.

Extensions

1. Take some or all of the words off the wall. Pass them out to students and have them put them back in their proper places. Make sure they explain why the word goes where they say.
2. Search for words on the wall that act as more than one part of speech. These searches can lead to great conversations about grammar.
3. Pick a word at random from the wall. Now students must make a sentence using that word as part of an original sentence. To make it more challenging, they can only add a word that comes from the categories to the left or the right of the original word.
4. Use the words in each category in other methods. For example, the conjunctions list can be powerful for expanding sentences used in other methods, or in students' independent writing.

Sample Grammar Wall

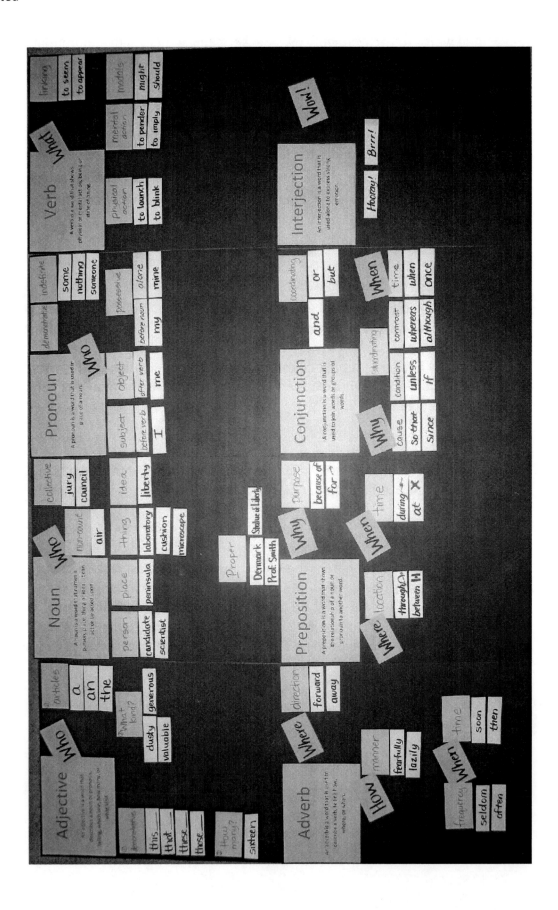

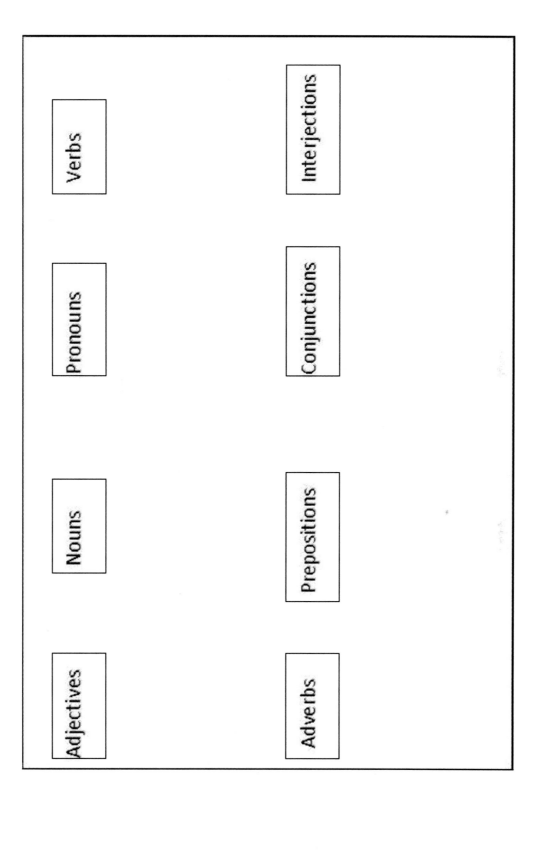

Grammar Wall

Verbs

Interjections

Pronouns

Conjunctions

Nouns

Prepositions

Adjectives

Adverbs

Parts of Speech

NOUN

A noun is a word that names a person, place, thing, or idea. It can act or be acted upon.

Examples: Roger, Father McGovern, the Yankees, bowlers, cousins, neighborhood, Baltimore, attic, Asia, Newark Airport, Golden Gate Bridge, glove, class, triangle, goodness, strength.

PRONOUN

A pronoun is a word that is used in place of a noun.

Examples: he, you, they, them, it, her, our, your, its, their, anybody, both, nobody, someone, several, himself, ourselves, themselves, yourself, itself, who, whom, which, what, whose.

ADJECTIVE

An adjective is a word that is used to describe a noun or pronoun, telling what kind, how many or which one.

Examples: green, enormous, slinky, original, Italian, some, few, eleven, all, none, that, this, these, those, third.

VERB

A verb is a word that shows physical or mental action, being, or state of being.

Examples: swayed, dance, think, imagine, love, approve, am, is, was, were, been, seems, appears, feels, remains.

ADVERB

An adverb is a word that is used to describe a verb, telling where, how, or when.

Examples: quietly, lovingly, skillfully, slyly, honestly, very, quite, extremely, too, moderately, seldom, never, often, periodically, forever.

PREPOSITION

A preposition is a word used to show the relationship of a noun or pronoun to another word.

Examples: across, below, toward, within, over, above, before, until, of, beyond, from, during, after, at, against.

CONJUNCTION

A conjunction is a word that is used to join words or groups of words.

Examples: and, or, either, neither, but, because, while, however, since, for.

INTERJECTION

An interjection is a word that is used alone to express strong emotion.

Examples: Heavens! Cheers! Oh! Aha! Darn!

Parts of Speech

Adjective	Noun
• Comparative/superlative • Articles • Demonstrative • Number • Observation/quality • Size • Shape • Age • Color • Origin • Material • Qualifier *Clauses	• Person, place, thing, idea (abstract) • Singular/plural • Irregular plural • Collective • Proper • Possessive • Compound • Non-count • Gerunds
Pronoun	**Verb**
• Personal subject • Personal object • Possessive • Demonstrative • Relative • Indefinite • Reflexive • Interrogative • Reciprocal	• Action • Linking • Helping/Modals • Irregular • Phrasal
Adverb	**Preposition**
• Manner • Direction • Frequency • Time • Intensifiers (Degree) *Clauses	• Time • Location • Purpose *Phrases
Conjunction	**Interjection**
• Coordinating • Subordinating (time, cause, condition, contrast) • Correlative	

Description
Students study a discrete grammar skill through a teacher-directed presentation, followed by collaborative and independent student tasks.

Purpose
Students need focused and direct instruction in the discrete elements of English grammar. This interactive method provides a step-by-step protocol for organizing grammar skill instruction. It can be used for everything from teaching simple adjectives before nouns to deictic pronoun use in scientific text! How's that for versatility?

Key Language Skills
Targeted parts of speech.

Materials
Chart paper, markers, sentence strip.

Procedures
1. Teacher prepares a *Grammar Study* Preview Chart that has the following components:

    a. Language objective written in a complete sentence

    b. Identification of the part, or parts, of speech that will be under study

    c. A general statement of why we are studying this. In other words, what will knowing this skill help students to do?

    d. Picture, or pictures, that will be used to "show" students the concept

    e. Two to three prepared sentences that prominently demonstrate how the specific grammar skill is actually used.

    f. A formula, written on sentence strip, that governs the use of the grammar skill.

Step 1: Using your preview chart, go through the items on it, in order.

Step 2: Construct one or two teacher-directed sentences using the skill to show students the application of the formula.

Step 3: Collaboratively, generate two or three sentences with the students. For some concepts, a picture or pictures, will be essential to helping students to understand and generate sentences using the skill.

Step 4: In pairs, have students create a single sentence that uses the skill. If applicable, they should follow the formula from the preview chart.

Step 5: Individually, have students create additional sentences following the same procedure as in step 4.

Step 6: Students can complete worksheets, or other pre-produced grammar support materials.

Hot Tips

1. The use of colored markers can go a long way to make concepts and relationships more clear.

2. Draw lines, arrows, and boxes to help students understand the physical relationship between the focused grammar skill you are teaching and other parts of speech that affect its use and application. For example, draw a colored arrow from an adjective to the noun it modifies.

3. Look for other methods you have used for examples of how this grammar skill has already been used.

Grammar Study Example

Preview Chart

Working Chart

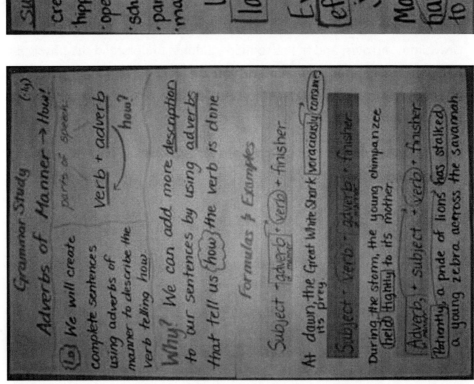

Twelve Basic Verb Tenses

Past	Present	Future
Simple Past Can use linking verbs (to be/to have)	**Simple Present** Can use linking verbs (to be/to have) Modal form	**Simple Future** Can use linking verbs (to be/to have)
Past Progressive	Present Progressive Modal form	Future Progressive
Past Perfect	Present Perfect Modal form	Future Perfect
Past Perfect Progressive	Present Perfect Progressive Modal form	Future Perfect Progressive

* All tenses can be written in the conditional and passive voice.

*Sentence types: declarative (w/ negative), interrogative, imperative, exclamatory.

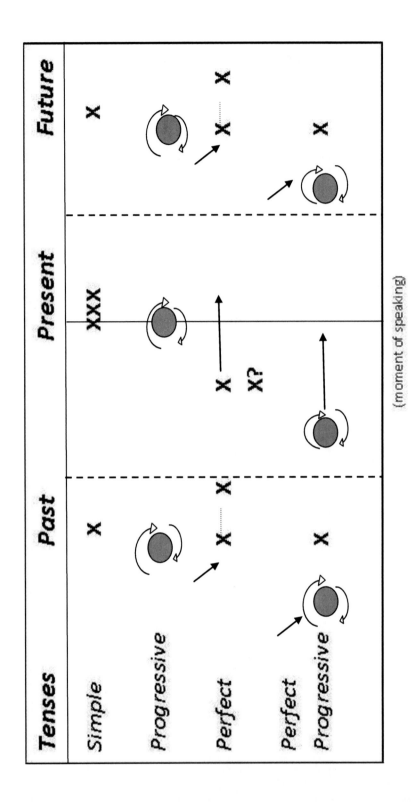

Verb Tense Timeline

Tenses	Past	Present	Future
Simple			
Progressive			
Perfect			
Perfect Progressive			

(moment of speaking)

Description

Students learn the form, meaning and use of different verb tenses through direct teaching of a particular tense by the teacher. These lessons usually unfold over several days, and are presented through the use of teacher-made charts or textbooks that clearly explain the tense, show how it is used, and explore how it serves to convey meaning. The use of graphic organizers, different color text and pictures help to support students as they work on mastering this important aspect of the English language.

Purpose

Of all the language skills, verb tense variety and control are usually the most lacking in English learners' language skills inventory. This strategy's purpose is to explicitly teach verb tenses in a particular order and with a specific plan.

Key Language Skills

Morphology, syntax

Materials

Chart paper, different color markers, quality color pictures measuring at least 5x7 inches.

General Procedures

1. Decide on your clear and specific verb tense teaching objective. Ensure that it logically follows from prior related instruction. For example, teaching the future tense before students understand the subject pronouns, or the present tense, will only complicate the lesson.

2. Ensure that your objective is written on your *Verb Tense Study* chart in a clear and specific sentence.

3. Select key examples sentences that show how the tense is used. Select language that students already know. Use complete sentences.

4. Use pictures to ensure comprehension. This is critical and not to be overlooked or neglected.

5. Use various colors on the chart to emphasize elements of the tense that are of high, medium or low importance.

6. Use arrows, squiggly lines and bubbles to relate words and concepts.

7. Ensure that the verb structure is illustrated with at least three complete sentences that demonstrate its form, use and meaning.

8. Build in several opportunities for students to practice the new tense. Use varied student groupings to maximize student language production (50-50 principle).

Step-by-Step Process

Step 1.

Create a *Verb Tense Study Preview Chart.* This chart will help you and your students to better comprehend and use each tense. This chart is completed by the teacher prior to the beginning of the verb tense study. It serves as your first introduction and direct lesson about the tense. It should be posted and serves as an on-going tool for you and your students. (Note the blank form of this *Preview Chart* on page 30).

Step 2:

Use pictures to determine subjects and verbs. Start with the declarative form. Select a picture and attach it to a piece of chart paper (the working chart).

   a. To the left of the picture, you and the students will generate subjects that are represented in the picture

   b. To the right of the picture, generate verbs that are represented in the picture. Write the verbs in the infinitive form. You should try for three to five subjects and verbs for each picture.

Step 3:

Collaboratively generate two to three sentences for each picture using a subject or two from the left, and one or more verbs from the right column. This is a time to review the formula and to ensure that the students "see" how the verb is conjugated in accord with the formula.

   a. There is no rush during this step. This is the "guided application" section and is critical.

   b. Other sentences may be generated in this fashion if they help students to better understand the formula, its application, and the real-world use of the tense.

Step 4:

<u>Paired sentence generation using the chart pictures.</u> Pair students and assign them the task of using one of the subjects on the left (that were not used in the collaborative sentences from Step 2) and one of the verbs from the right (same requirement). They are to formulate a sentence that follow the verb tense formula.

Step 5:

<u>Students create individual sentences similar to the process in Step 4,</u> and/or they complete focused worksheets on the verb tense under study.

This five-step process then repeats itself for the next form (negative, interrogative, imperative) form of the verb.

Hot Tips

1. Of all the hot tips, this is the most powerful: <u>put the charts up on the wall of your classroom and refer to them often.</u> They must become "living" guides for students as they navigate the sometimes complex world of verbs and their tenses.

2. Think of creative ways to review the formulas. For example, give students parts of the formula and have them line up in the correct order. Take sentences from other school materials and find the parts of the formula in them.

3. Consider devoting a partial lesson every week to reviewing prior *Verb Tense Studies*. In this way, students keep integrating new tenses with prior ones.

Extensions

1. Use the verb tense you are working on as part of other language-building activities, including writing tasks to reinforce verb tenses within the total grammar system of the English language.

2. Keep a running list of the verb tenses your students have studied. Have them supply good examples for each tense.

3. Have students make a verb tense book to use as a guide as they work on various writing or reading tasks.

Verb Tense Study Example

Working Chart

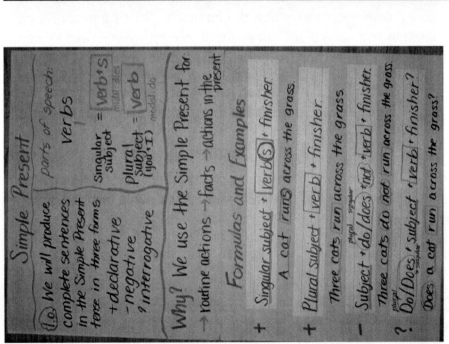

Subjects
Singular
- Camper
- curious neighbor

Plural
- young scientists
- brother and sister
- Siblings
- explorers and their dog

Verbs
- to observe
- to wander
- to search for
- to explore
- to wonder
  about ____

Every fall, the curious neighbor wanders through the forest with his binoculars and guide dog.

The young scientists wonder about the local wildlife as they walk along the path.

Every year, the explorers and their dog search for leaves changing color as soon as autumn begins.

Preview Chart

Simple Present

parts of speech: Verbs

1.) We will produce complete sentences in the Simple Present tense in three forms
+ declarative
− negative
? interrogative

Singular subject = verb + s
Plural subject (you + I) = verb

Why? We use the Simple Present for
→ routine actions → facts → actions in the present

Formulas and Examples

+ Singular subject + verb(s) + finisher.
A cat runs across the grass.

+ Plural subject + verb + finisher.
Three cats run across the grass.

− Subject + do/does + not + verb + finisher.
Three cats do not run across the grass.

? Do/Does + subject + verb + finisher?
Does a cat run across the grass?

Grammar Study/ Verb Tense Study
Blank Template

(Title)

Language Objective:	Parts of Speech:

Application (Why?):

Formulas & Examples

(Formula 1)

(Example 1)

(Formula 2)

(Example 2)

(Formula 3)

(Example 3)

Monitoring Your Verb Tense Study

Does the chart have the following essential components?

Component	Yes	No
Language Objective		
Parts of Speech		
Application/Why		
Formulas		
Examples		
Picture for Brainstorming		
Brainstorming		
Collaborative Sentences		
Is it done on a piece of chart paper large enough for the class to see?		

Incorporating PUSH! in the *Verb Tense Study*

Below are various *PUSHES!* that should guide the design and implementation of this method.

Subjects	Example
Singular Common	A dog…
Plural Common	Six firefighters…
Proper, Singular and Plural	Governor Jones…
Compound	The teacher and her students…
Preceded by an adjective	The *newborn* puppies…
Human subjects + "who …"	The man *who* is standing near the car…
Inanimate subjects + "that…"	The van *that* tipped over…
Subjects + "with…"	The students *with* their backs to the camera…

Verbs	Example
Common physical action	to jump, to run, to sit
Content-related physical action	to dissect, to observe, to fumigate
Irregular	to arise, to break, to stand
Phrasal	to act like, to back up, to do over
Transitive	to wash (the car), to take (a ride) , to study (math)
Reflexive	To enjoy oneself, to hurt oneself
Mental action	to think, to ponder, to plan
State of Being	am, is, are, was, were, be, been, being, (ex., to be worried, to be shocked)
Bloom's Taxonomy Type	to analyze, to hypothesize, to evaluate

Types of Sentences

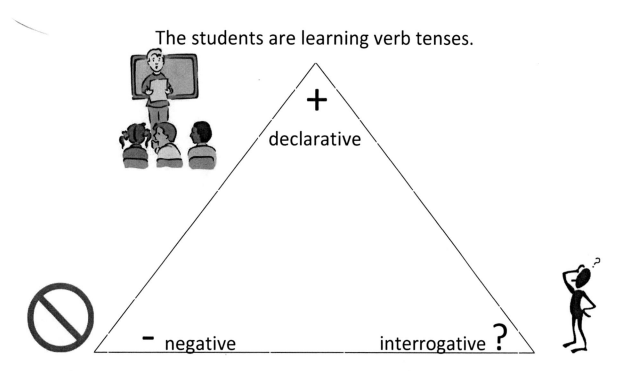

The students are learning verb tenses.

+ declarative

− negative

interrogative ?

The students are **not** learning verb tenses.

Are the students learning verb tenses?

Type of sentence	Use	Punctuation	Example
Declarative	Telling sentence	.	The dog runs.
Negative (declarative)	"No" sentence	.	The dog does not run.
Interrogative	Asking sentence	?	Does the dog run?
Imperative	Command	.	Chase the dog please.
Exclamatory	Excitement	!	Wow! The dog runs fast!

Nouns

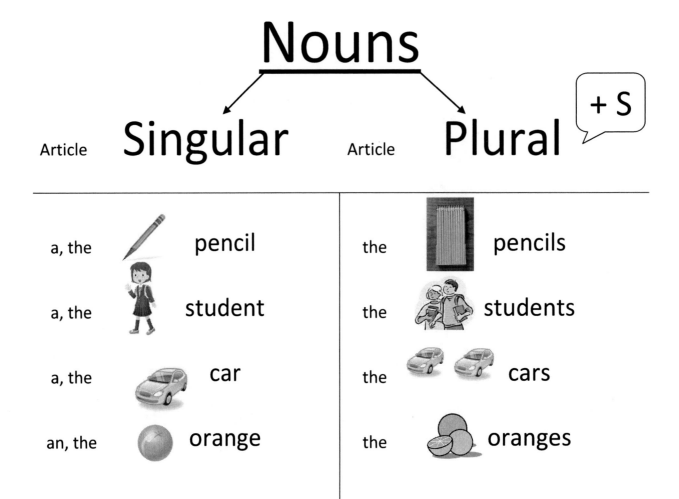

Article	Singular	Article	Plural	+ S
a, the	pencil	the	pencils	
a, the	student	the	students	
a, the	car	the	cars	
an, the	orange	the	oranges	

Verbs

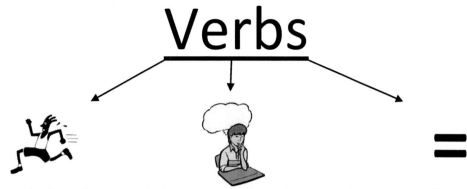

Physical Action	Mental Action	State of Being
• To jump	• To think	**To be**
• To fly	• To acknowledge____	am is are
• To sprint	• To accept____	was were
• To land	• To comprehend____	will be
• To blink	• To evaluate_____	being been
• To hover	• To analyze_____	**Other Linking Verbs**
• To catch____	• To concentrate	• To seem____
• To scrape____	• To compare_____	• To appear_____
• To sprinkle____	• To ponder_____	• To become_____
• To crush_____	• To imagine_____	• To turn_____
• To lunge	• To estimate_____	• To grow_____
• To growl	• To enjoy_____	• To feel_____
• To salute_____	• To discern____	• To sound____
• To ignite_____	• To judge_____	• To look_____

*Blanks after the verb ("to compare____") signify that the verb is normally used as a transitive verb meaning that it requires an object (nous or pronouns) after it ("to compare ideas"). Conversely, intransitive verbs ("to growl") are fine without an object afterward.

Pronouns & To be Verbs

Personal Subject Pronoun	_Past_	_Present_	_Future_
I	was	am	will be
you	were	are	will be
he	was	is	will be
she	was	is	will be
it	was	is	will be
we	were	are	will be
you	were	are	will be
they	were	are	will be

Singular (brace grouping I, you, he, she, it)

Plural (brace grouping we, you, they)

Pronoun Pictures by Joel D. Castro

Basic Verb Tense Studies

- To be Verbs in the Present
- To be Verbs in the Past
- To be Verbs in the Future
- Has, Have, Had
- Present Progressive
- Past Progressive
- Future Progressive
- Simple Present
- Simple Past
- Irregular Past
- Simple Future
- Modals: can, may, might, must
- Infinitive Verbs: "used to ___" and "going to ____"
- Present Perfect

Am, Is, Are

(To be verbs in the Present)

Language Objective:	Parts of Speech:
We will write complete sentences using am, is, or are to connect the subject to adjectives in three forms: -declarative, -negative, -interrogative.	*Verbs* ↓ I: **am** singular subject: **is** plural subject/you: **are**

Application (Why?):

We use **am, is,** and **are** to:

- give facts,
- talk about the present,
- connect the subject to an adjective that describes it.

Formulas & Examples

Declarative

Subject + am/is/are + finisher (adjective).

Example

Zebras are black and white with stripes.

Negative

Subject + am/is/are + (not) + finisher (adjective).

Example

A household pet, like a cat or dog, is (not) wild.

Interrogative

Am/Is/Are + subject + finisher (adjective)?

Example

Is the weather warm and sunny?

To be Verbs

*Notes

1. This can be a challenging verb tense for students as no action is shown. Rather, the "to be" verbs act like equal signs, equating the subject to the adjective that follows. In the examples given, the "to be" verbs are linking verbs that link the subject to the subject complement, the adjective.

2. To help your students understand this construction, try setting up your working chart in the following way. (All tenses of the "to be" verbs can be set up this way.)

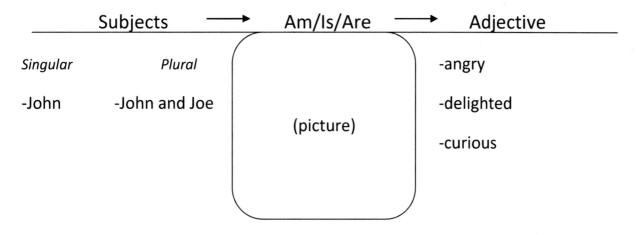

Subjects	→	Am/Is/Are	→	Adjective

Singular	Plural		
-John	-John and Joe	(picture)	-angry
			-delighted
			-curious

Basic Time Markers

Try adding these to your sentences to provide more detail.

Past	Present	Future
• Yesterday	• Today	• Tomorrow
• Earlier	• Now	• Later
• Last _____	• Right now	• Next _____

Was/Were
(To be verbs in the Past)

Language Objective:	**Parts of Speech:**
We will write complete sentences using was or were to connect the subject to adjectives in three forms: -declarative, -negative, -interrogative.	*Verbs* ↓ singular subject/I: **was** plural subject/you: **were**

Application (Why?):
We use **was** and **were** to:
- talk about the past,
- connect the subject to an adjective that describes it.

Formulas & Examples

Declarative

Subject + was/were + finisher (adjective).

Example

Yesterday's exam was difficult but short.

Negative

Subject + was/were + (not) + finisher (adjective).

Example

Many students were(not)ready for the test last week.

Interrogative

Was/Were + subject + finisher (adjective)?

Example

Was the teacher concerned about the students' performance on the assessment?

Will be
(To be verb in the Future)

Language Objective:	Parts of Speech:
We will write complete sentences using "will be" to connect the subject to adjectives in three forms: -declarative, -negative, -interrogative.	*Verbs + Finishers* ↓ **will be** + adjectives nouns prepositional phrases

Application (Why?):
We use **will be** to:
- talk about the future,
- connect the subject to an adjective, prepositional phrase or noun.

Formulas & Examples

Declarative

Subject + will be + finisher.

Example

Tomorrow will be rainy and cloudy.

Negative

Subject + will + (not) + be finisher.

Example

Your science projects will (not) be in the library next week.

Interrogative

Will + subject + be + finisher?

Example

Will Juan be the line leader for the whole month?

Has, Have, Had

Language Objective:	Parts of Speech:
We will write complete sentences using has, have, or had to connect the subject to nouns in two forms: -declarative, -negative.	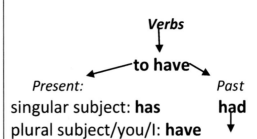 *Verbs* **to have** *Present:* *Past* singular subject: **has** **had** plural subject/you/I: **have** modals: does, do did

Application (Why?):

We use **has** and **have** to show possession in the present.

We use **had** to show possession in the past.

Formulas & Examples

Declarative

Subject + has/have/had + finisher (noun/noun phrase).

Example

Zoo animals have large cages so that they can roam freely.

Negative

Subject + does/do/did + (not) + have + finisher (noun/noun phrase).

Example

Last year, the museum's exhibits did not have protective glass windows.

Has, Have, Had

*Notes

1. This can be a challenging verb tense for students as no action is shown. Rather the verb "to have" functions to show possession.

2. To help your students understand this construction, try setting up your working chart in the following way.

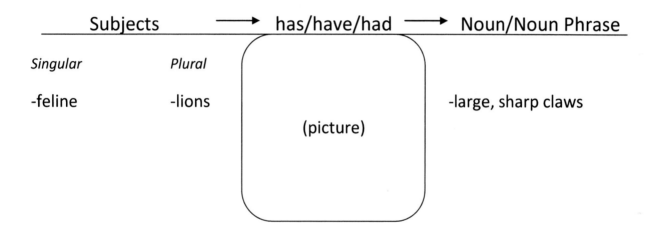

Subjects	⟶	has/have/had	⟶	Noun/Noun Phrase

Singular   *Plural*

-feline   -lions   (picture)   -large, sharp claws

Present Progressive

<table>
<tr>
<td>

Language Objective:
We will write complete sentences in the present progressive verb tense in three forms:
-declarative,
-negative,
-interrogative.

</td>
<td>

Parts of Speech:

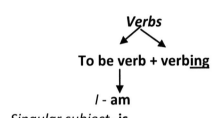

Verbs

To be verb + verbing

I - **am**
Singular subject- **is**
Plural subject/you- **are**

</td>
</tr>
</table>

Application (Why?):
We use the present progressive to show actions that are:
- happening in the present time and are
- ongoing.

Formulas & Examples

Declarative

Subject + am/is/are + verbing + finisher.

Example

At the moment, the students are diligently studying for their upcoming exam.

Negative

Subject + am/is/are + not + verbing + finisher.

Example

Surprisingly, the temperamental dog is not barking at the mail carrier right now.

Interrogative

Am/Is/Are + subject + verbing + finisher?

Example

Are they waiting for their teacher to arrive before they enter the classroom?

Progressive Tenses

*Notes

1. Students need to understand that the –ing ending is what indicates an ongoing action. Below are some helpful time markers that help to indicate progression.

Progressive Time Markers

Try adding these to your sentences to provide more detail.

Past	Present	Future
• Yesterday	• Today	• Tomorrow
• Earlier	• Now	• Later
• Last _____	• Right now	• Next _____
• For ___ (time period)	• For ___ (time period)	• For ___ (time period)
• During _____	• At this moment	• During _____
• Before____	• Currently	• After____
• A while ago	• Presently	• Soon

Past Progressive

Language Objective: We will write complete sentences in the past progressive verb tense in three forms: -declarative, -negative, -interrogative.	Parts of Speech: *Verbs* **To be verb + verbing** *Singular subject/I-* **was** *Plural subject/you-* **were**

Application (Why?):
We use the past progressive to show actions that were:
- happening in the past and were
- ongoing.

Formulas & Examples

Declarative

Subject + was/were + verbing + finisher.

Example

A group of responsible students was preparing for their test yesterday.

Negative

Subject + was/were + not + verbing + finisher.

Example

This morning, two children were not playing outside with the rest of the class.

Interrogative

Was/Were + subject + verbing + finisher?

Example

Was the busy flight attendant serving refreshments during the flight?

Future Progressive

Language Objective:	Parts of Speech:
We will write complete sentences in the future progressive verb tense in three forms: -declarative, -negative, -interrogative.	*Verbs*  **To be verb + verb<u>ing</u>** *(All subjects)* **will be**

Application (Why?):
We use the future progressive to show actions that will be:
- happening in the future and will be
- ongoing.

Formulas & Examples

Declarative

Subject + │ will be │ + │verbing│ + finisher.

Example

Flocks of birds │will be│ │migrating│ during the winter months.

Negative

Subject + │will│ + <u>not</u> + │be│ + │verbing│ + finisher.

Example

Next year, retail stores │will│ │not│ be │hiring│ as many employees.

Interrogative

│Will│ + subject + │be│ + │verbing│ + finisher?

Example

│Will│ drivers │be│ │consuming│ as much gasoline during the summer travel season?

Simple Present

Language Objective:	Parts of Speech:
We will write complete sentences in the simple present verb tense in three forms: -declarative, -negative, -interrogative.	*Verbs* ↓ singular subject- **verb(s)** plural subject- **verb** (I/you) *modals:* singular subject- **does** plural subject/I/you- **do**

Application (Why?):

We use the Simple Present to show actions that:
- happen routinely,
- happen in the present,
- are simple facts.

Formulas & Examples

Declarative

Singular Subject + verb(s) + finisher.

Plural Subject + verb + finisher.

Example

The young girl brushes her teeth every morning.

The young girl and her brother brush their teeth every morning.

Negative

Subject + does/do + not + verb + finisher.

Example

Herbivores do not eat meat.

Interrogative

Does/Do + subject + verb + finisher?

Example

Does your neighbor walk her dog daily?

Simple Present

*Notes

1. Simple present can be a particularly troublesome tense for students. For beginning students, consider extending the time spent on this tense. The following schedule is helpful for younger and beginning level students.

- Declarative with singular subjects

- Declarative with plural subjects

-Declarative with both singular and plural subjects

-Negative

-Interrogative

-Review as needed

2. Simple present is used in academic text to show routine actions or simple facts. Consider using the following time markers to help students understand the application.

Simple Present Time Markers

- Every day

- Every _____

- During _____

- Always

- Routinely

- Habitually

- Consistently

Simple Past

<table>
<tr>
<td colspan="2">

Language Objective:
We will write complete sentences in the simple past verb tense in three forms:
-declarative,
-negative,
-interrogative.

</td>
<td>

Parts of Speech:

Verbs
↓

verb(ed)

modal: did

</td>
</tr>
<tr>
<td colspan="3">

Application (Why?):
We use the simple past to show actions that:
• happened in the past.

</td>
</tr>
<tr>
<td colspan="3">

Formulas & Examples

</td>
</tr>
<tr>
<td>*Declarative*</td>
<td colspan="2">

Subject + verbed + finisher.

</td>
</tr>
<tr>
<td>*Example*</td>
<td colspan="2">

Last year, scientists discovered many new species of insects.

</td>
</tr>
<tr>
<td>*Negative*</td>
<td colspan="2">

Subject + did + not + verb + finisher.

</td>
</tr>
<tr>
<td>*Example*</td>
<td colspan="2">

For a long time, astronomers did not believe the earth revolved around the sun.

</td>
</tr>
<tr>
<td>*Interrogative*</td>
<td colspan="2">

Did + subject + verb + finisher?

</td>
</tr>
<tr>
<td>*Example*</td>
<td colspan="2">

Did cartographers create new maps when Hawaii became a state?

</td>
</tr>
</table>

Simple Past

(Regular and Irregular)

*Notes

1. Teach the simple past (-ed) ending and irregular past separately. This means that students will need to be directed to specific verbs to use. Example: Don't use "to drive" on the simple past chart as it does not take on the "-ed" ending in the past tense.

2. **Irregular Past**: With over 200 verbs that do not take the "-ed" ending in the past, students will need to be provided with a resource list of the present and past tense forms of the verb. This is a good time to introduce a list with:

- Infinitive form,

- Past Tense form,

- Past Participle form (to be added to when Present Perfect is taught).

  ○ See example below.

Infinitive Form	Simple Past	Past Participle With: have, has, or had
• To see	• Saw	
• To run	• Ran	*(Leave this third column on your chart blank. During the instruction of the Present Perfect, you will fill in this Past Participle column. To see the completed chart, turn to page 57.)*
• To read	• Read	
• To swim	• Swam	
• To go	• Went	
• To drive	• Drove	
• To drink	• Drank	
• To eat	• Ate	

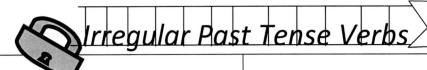

Irregular Past Tense Verbs

Some Past Tense Verbs break the rules!

Language Objective: We will write complete sentences using irregular past tense verbs in three forms: -declarative, -negative, -interrogative.	**Parts of Speech:** *Verbs* ↓ **Irregular Verbs** do not take -ed in the past tense. -ed

Application (Why?):

We add –ed to most verbs to show the past tense, but we don't add –ed to **irregular past tense verbs**. They have special endings or don't change at all.

Formulas & Examples

Declarative:

Subject + irregular verb + finisher.

Example:

As soon as she got home, the teenager ran outside, dove into the pool and then swam from one end to the other.

Negative:

Subject + did + not + base verb + finisher.

Example:

I did not speak for two days when I had laryngitis.

Interrogative:

Did + subject + base verb + finisher?

Example:

Did the toddler really sleep, or did she just shut her eyes?

Simple Future

Language Objective:	Parts of Speech:
We will write complete sentences in the simple future verb tense in three forms: -declarative, -negative, -interrogative.	*Verbs* **will + verb**

Application (Why?):

We use the simple future to show actions that will:

- happen in the future.

Formulas & Examples

Declarative

Subject + will + verb + finisher.

Example

Tadpoles will hatch from their eggs in the coming spring.

Negative

Subject + will + not + verb + finisher.

Example

The next solar eclipse will not occur for many years.

Interrogative

Will + subject + verb + finisher?

Example

Will archeologists discover new dinosaur fossils in the future?

Modals: can, may, might, must

Language Objective:	Parts of Speech:
We will write complete sentences using the modals can, might, may, and must in three forms: -declarative, -negative, -interrogative.	Verbs ➔ Modals **Can:** shows ability **May:** shows permission or chance **Might:** shows possibility or chance **Must:** shows requirement **modal + verb**

Application (Why?):
We use modals before the verb to add a very specific meaning to the verb.

Formulas & Examples

Declarative

Subject + modal + verb + finisher.

Example

The storm might cause the power to go out.

Negative

Subject + modal + not + verb + finisher.

Example

Children must not play outside during lightning storms.

Interrogative

Modal + subject + verb + finisher?

Example

May the students walk home in the rain if they use their umbrellas?

Modals

*Notes

1. Modals are presented twice on the Preview Charts. In this section, "can," "may," "might," and "must" are introduced. As an extension try adding, "have to," "ought to," and "shall."

2. Modals are significant in that they add very specific meaning to the sentence. It's important that students understand how these small words change the mood of the entire sentence, and how and when to use each. Try switching the modal in a sentence to see how the meaning changes.

Example: Students **must** study during recess.

Students **may** study during recess.

Students **can** study during recess.

Students **might** study during recess.

Used to_____ & Going to _____

Language Objective: We will write complete sentences using "used to" and "going to" before base verbs.	**Parts of Speech:** *Verb Phrases* ↓ used to + base verb **or** going to + base verb

Application (Why?):
We use the "used to" and "going to" in informal speech for:
- Used to: a past habit that is now over,
- Going to: a future action that has not yet happened.

Formulas & Examples

Formula

Subject + used to + base verb + finisher.

Example

When the actress was younger, she used to practice her lines in front of a mirror.

Formula

Subject + to be verb + going to + base verb + finisher.

Example

Later this week, the critics are going to review the new play.

Used to and Going to

*Notes

1. These two structures are common ways of expressing past or future actions without using the formal past and future tenses.

Time Markers

Used to	*Going to*
(time in past, but can't be a specific time)	(must be time in future)
• When I was _____ (young, a child, in high school, etc.)	• Next _____ (week, month, year, etc.)
	• Later
• Every _____ (day, week, month, etc.)	• In _____ (May, an hour, etc.)

Present Perfect

Language Objective:	Parts of Speech:
We will write complete sentences in the present perfect verb tense in three forms: -declarative, -negative, -interrogative.	*Verbs* ↙ ↘ **has/have + past participle** singular subject- **has** plural subject- **have** (I/you)

Application (Why?):
We use the present perfect to show actions that:
- have recently ended,
- started in the past but may continue in the present,
- happened in the past but the time is unknown or unimportant (relate an experience).

Formulas & Examples

Declarative

Subject + has/have + past participle + finisher.

Example

The neighboring countries have battled over the disputed territory for centuries.

Negative

Subject + has/have + not + past participle + finisher.

Example

The President has not spoken to the public since last month.

Interrogative

Has/Have + subject + past participle + finisher?

Example

Have rescuers found the missing divers yet?

Present Perfect

*Notes

1. Present perfect is a challenging verb tense for students and teachers alike. Although a present tense, it's most often used to convey an action that began in the past. However, this action may continue into the current time (I have taught ELD for ten years.), have been recently completed (I have written my sentence.), or be used if the speaker is merely trying to communicate an experience without using a specific time marker (I have traveled to Mexico).

2. Past participles can also be challenging. Often times, they take the same form as the Simple Past: add –ed. However, the irregular forms have their own endings. To assist students, keep a running list of past participles. If the class started a list of irregular verbs, past participles can be added there. See the example below.

Infinitive Form	Simple Past	Past Participle With: have, has, or had
• To see	• Saw	• Seen
• To run	• Ran	• Run
• To read	• Read	• Read
• To swim	• Swam	• Swum
• To go	• Went	• Gone
• To drive	• Drove	• Driven
• To drink	• Drank	• Drunk
• To eat	• Ate	• Eaten

Present Perfect Time Markers

- since_____
- for _____

Basic Grammar Studies

- Adjectives before the Noun (What kind?)
- Adjectives before the Noun (How many?)
- Proper Nouns
- Irregular Plural Nouns
- Prepositions of Location
- Prepositions of Time
- Subject and Object Pronouns
- Possessive Nouns
- Possessive Pronouns
- Coordinating Conjunctions: and, or, but
- Comparative Adjectives
- Superlative Adjectives
- Adverbs of Manner
- Demonstrative Adjectives/Pronouns

Adjectives before the Noun

What kind?

Language Objective: We will write complete sentences using adjectives that tell "what kind" before nouns to add detail.	**Parts of Speech:** *Adjectives* *(What Kind?)* Adjective ⟶ **Noun** *What kind?* *Quality *Age *Material *Size *Color *Qualifier *Shape *Origin

Application (Why?):
We use adjectives that tell what kind to describe the nouns that follow.

Formulas & Examples

Formula:

Adjective + (noun) + verb + finisher.

Example:

Ancient redwoods grow in California.

Formula:

Adjective 1 + adjective 2 + (noun) + verb + finisher.

Example:

Colonial American flags had only thirteen stars.

Adjectives before the Noun- What kind?

*Notes

1. Adjectives before nouns are generally sequenced in this order: Which one? (articles and demonstratives), How many?(quantity), What kind? (everything else: observation, size, shape, age, color, origin, material, qualifier).

2. The "qualifier" adjective is considered the most significant attribute about the noun, the one that defines it most closely. For example, in describing a piece of jewelry, such as a ring, with the adjectives, "diamond," "expensive," and "engagement," the order would be *expensive* (observation) *diamond* (material) *engagement* (qualifier) *ring*. "Engagement" would be considered the qualifier as it most clearly defines and distinguishes the ring from other rings.

3. For the working chart for adjectives that answer "What kind?" and "How many?" use the following setup to reflect the formula. Generate subjects and verbs **first** and then go back to describe the subjects with corresponding adjectives.

Adjectives	Subjects		Verbs
-sleek	-jets		-to take off
-silver		(picture)	
-fighter			

Adjectives before the Noun

How many?

	Parts of Speech:
Language Objective: We will write complete sentences using adjectives that tell "how many" before nouns to add detail.	***Adjectives*** **Adjective ⟶ Noun** *How many?* <u>Definite</u> <u>Indefinite</u> two some nineteen few one thousand several

Application (Why?):
We use adjectives that tell how many to tell us the number of nouns that follow.

Formulas & Examples

Formula:

Adjective + noun + verb + finisher.

Example:

Every citizen should vote in the upcoming election.

Formula:

Adjective 1 + noun 1 + verb + adjective 2 + noun 2 + finisher.

Example:

Thirteen stripes decorate the American flag, indicating the few original colonies.

Adjectives before the Noun- How many?

*Notes

1. Adjectives before nouns are generally sequenced in this order: Which one? (articles and demonstratives), How many?(quantity), What kind? (everything else: observation, size, shape, age, color, origin, material, qualifier).

2. For adjectives that answer the question, "How many?," also known as adjectives of quantity, can be divided into definite and indefinite amounts. Students should be encouraged to use both. See the examples below.

How many?

Definite	*Indefinite*
• four	• some
• twelve	• many
• 700	• few
• one million	• several
• two thirds of…	• any

Proper Nouns

Language Objective:	Parts of Speech:
We will write complete sentences using proper nouns as the subject and object in declarative sentences.	*Nouns* **Proper Nouns** (Specific) 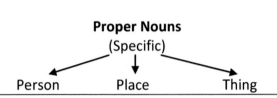 Person Place Thing

Application (Why?):
We use proper nouns to name specific people, places, things and ideas.

Formulas & Examples

Formula:

Proper Noun + verb + finisher.

Example:

Alaska is the largest state in the country.

Formula:

Subject + verb + Proper Noun + finisher.

Example:

Our country's longest river is the Mississippi River.

Proper Nouns

*Notes

1. For the working chart, it's important that students understand how to take a common noun and change it to a proper noun, a specifically named noun. Setup the working chart in the following way to show the transition from common to proper noun.

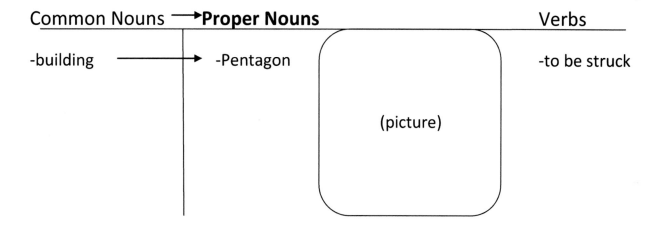

© Innovative Grammar 2010

65

No part of this book may be reproduced without explicit written permission of the authors.

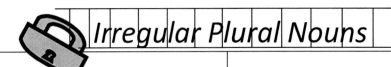

Irregular Plural Nouns

Some Plural Nouns break the rules!

Language Objective:
We will write complete sentences using irregular plural nouns as the subject and as the object in declarative sentences.

Parts of Speech:
Nouns
Irregular Plural Nouns

Do not take –s to make plurals.

Application (Why?):
We add –s to most nouns to change them from singular to plural, but we don't add –s to **irregular plural nouns**. They have special endings or don't change at all.

Formulas & Examples

Formula:

Irregular plural noun + verb + finisher.

Example:

Our front teeth are used for cutting and biting.

Formula:

Subject + verb + irregular plural noun + finisher.

Example:

I counted seventy-six sheep before I fell asleep last night.

Irregular Plural Nouns

*Notes

1. Because the focus of this *Grammar Study* is the irregular form of the noun, neither the verb nor verb tense has been specified. Depending on students' language level, a verb tense does not have to designated by the teacher OR students can review and practice a previously learned verb tense.

2. Due to the large number of irregular plural nouns, students will need a resource list. The list can be added to as more plural nouns are discussed. See the example below.

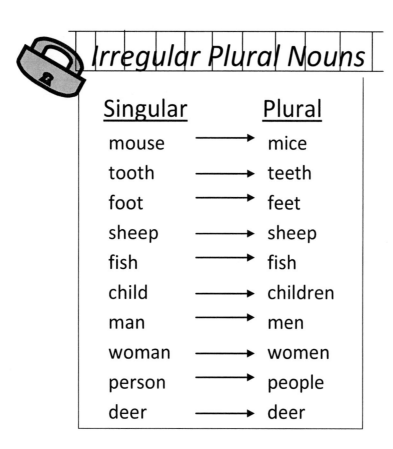

Irregular Plural Nouns	
Singular	Plural
mouse	mice
tooth	teeth
foot	feet
sheep	sheep
fish	fish
child	children
man	men
woman	women
person	people
deer	deer

Prepositions of Location

Where?

Language Objective: We will write complete sentences using prepositional phrases of location at the beginning and end of the sentence.	**Parts of Speech:** *Prepositions* _____ + _____ = prepositional phrase *preposition* *noun* → **Where?**

Application (Why?):
We use prepositions of location to relate to nouns and tell us **where.**

Formulas & Examples

Formula:

Subject + verb + finisher + prepositional phrase.

Example:

When the shark approached, the school of fish swam into the coral.

Formula:

Prepositional Phrase + subject + verb + finisher.

Example:

Beneath the sand, the hungry stingray awaited its prey.

Prepositions of Location

*Notes

1. Both prepositions of time and prepositions of location will be used in prepositional phrases meaning that the prepositions will be followed by nouns or noun phrases. Use the following setup for the working chart to clarify the sentence construction for students.

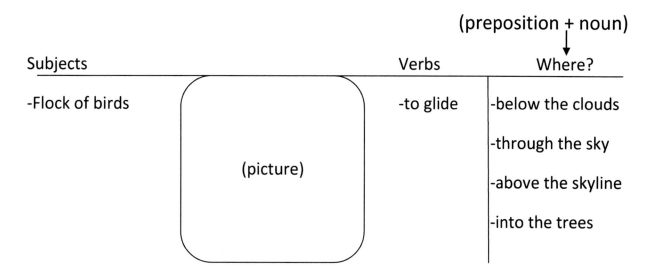

(preposition + noun)

Subjects	(picture)	Verbs	Where?
-Flock of birds		-to glide	-below the clouds
			-through the sky
			-above the skyline
			-into the trees

2. The commonly used prepositions of time, **in**, **on**, and **at** can be very difficult for students to use correctly. Consider the following general rules.

in *inside a space*	on *associated with something which has a surface*	at *neither within a space nor associated with a surface / something that someone is using*
• cities (Los Angeles) • continents (Africa) • countries (Spain) • rooms (kitchen) • buildings (greenhouse) • geographical areas (mountains, valleys) • objects (purse)	• parts of a house (steps, roof, floor, table) • bodies of water if you're not within in them (ocean, lake, Mississippi River)	• things being used (gym, desk, library) • general events (race, Olympics, car wash, movies)

Prepositions of Time

When?

Language Objective:	**Parts of Speech:**
We will write complete sentences using prepositional phrases of time at the beginning and end of the sentence.	*Prepositions*

In the Parts of Speech box:

_____ + _____ = prepositional phrase

preposition   *noun*

When?

Application (Why?):

We use prepositions of location to relate to nouns and tell us **when**.

Formulas & Examples

Formula:

Subject + verb + finisher + prepositional phrase.

Example:

The airplane passenger's luggage must be secured under her seat before take-off.

Formula:

Prepositional Phrase + subject + verb + finisher.

Example:

During the storm, the fishing boat rocked back and forth on the waves.

Prepositions of Time

*Notes

1. Both prepositions of time and prepositions of location will be used in prepositional phrases meaning that the prepositions will be followed by nouns or noun phrases. Use the following setup for the working chart to clarify the sentence construction for students.

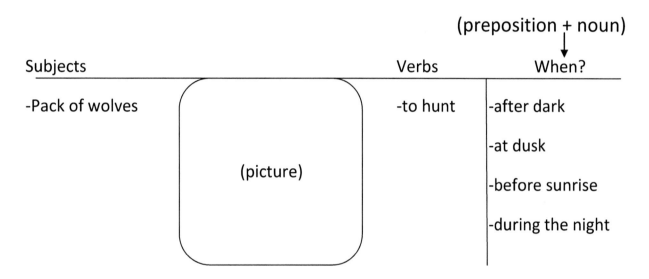

(preposition + noun)

Subjects		Verbs	When?
-Pack of wolves	(picture)	-to hunt	-after dark
			-at dusk
			-before sunrise
			-during the night

2. The commonly used prepositions of time, **in**, **on**, and **at** can be very difficult for students to use correctly. Consider the following general rules.

in	**on**	**at**
long periods of time	*specific dates and days*	*exact times*
<ul><li>months (September)</li><li>seasons (winter)</li><li>decades (1950s)</li><li>centuries (14th)</li><li>eras (Middle Ages)</li><li>general time (past)</li><li>most parts of day (morning, evening, afternoon)</li></ul>	<ul><li>days of week (Monday)</li><li>dates (April 15th)</li><li>holidays (Halloween)</li></ul>	<ul><li>time (2:30 pm)</li><li>short part of day (sunrise)</li><li>part of schedule (dinner, bedtime)</li><li>"night"</li></ul>

Personal Subject and Object Pronouns

Replace personal nouns!

Language Objective:	Parts of Speech:
We will write complete sentences using subject pronouns and object pronouns in three forms: 1. Subject pronouns before the verb, 2. Object pronouns after the verb, 3. Subject pronouns before the verb AND object pronouns after the verb.	**Pronouns** **Subject** (before the verb) / **Object** (after the verb) I — me you — you he, she, it — him, her, it we — us they — them

Application (Why?):

We use personal pronouns to replace nouns and avoid repetition.

- Subject pronouns replace nouns before the verb.
- Object pronouns replace nouns after the verb.

Formulas & Examples

Subject Pronoun Formula

Subject pronoun + verb + finisher.

Example

Old sentence: My sister and I walk to school every day.

New sentence: We walk to school every day.

Object Pronoun Formula

Subject + verb + finisher with object pronoun.

Example

Old sentence: Next week, the students will send letters to their former teacher.

New sentence: Next week the students will send letters to her.

Combined Formula

Subject pronoun + verb + finisher with object pronoun.

Example

Old sentence: Mr. Jones doesn't like to wash his car very often.

New sentence: He doesn't like to wash it very often.

Personal Subject and Object Pronouns

*Notes

1. For this *Grammar Study*, students must understand the connection between the subject nouns and the pronouns that replace them. See the following working chart setups for subject and object pronouns.

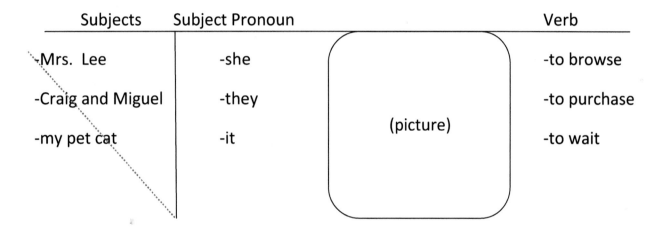

Subjects	Subject Pronoun		Verb
-Mrs. Lee	-she	(picture)	-to browse
-Craig and Miguel	-they		-to purchase
-my pet cat	-it		-to wait

Subjects		Verbs + Object	Object Pronoun
-Circus performers	(picture)	-to toss <u>the acrobat</u>	-her
- elephant		-to obey <u>the trainer</u>	-him
-clown		-to entertain <u>the crowd</u>	-us

Possessive Nouns

<table>
<tr>
<td rowspan="1">

Language Objective:
We will write complete sentences using singular and plural possessive nouns.

</td>
<td>

Parts of Speech:
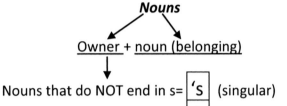

Nouns

Owner + noun (belonging)

Nouns that do NOT end in s= | **'s** | (singular)

Nouns that end in s= | **'** | (plural)

</td>
</tr>
</table>

Application (Why?):
We use possessive nouns to show possession.
We add **'s** to nouns that don't end in **s.**
We add **just the apostrophe (')** to nouns that do end in **s.**

Formulas & Examples

Singular Formula

Singular noun + 's + (noun) + verb + finisher.

Example

The bicycle's (front tire) is flat.

Plural Formula

Plural noun + ' + (noun) + verb + finisher.

Example

All the toddlers' (tricycles) have three wheels.

Possessive Nouns

*Notes

1. Possessive nouns are not restricted to only the subject of the sentence. (Example: The yellow fur ball under the couch is Jessica's cat.) Possessive nouns will either precede the noun of which they have possession, or stand in for the noun. (Example: The yellow cat is Jessica's.).

2. Consider the following setup for the working chart. First generate the subjects and then the owners of the subjects.

Owner	Subjects (belongings)		Verb
-California's	-poppies		-to bloom
- city's	-residents	(picture)	-to vote

Possessive Pronouns

Language Objective:	Parts of Speech:
We will write complete sentences using possessive pronouns before the noun and independently.	**Pronouns** <table><tr><td>**Who does it belong to?**</td><td>**Before noun**</td><td>**Independently**</td></tr><tr><td>Me</td><td>my_____</td><td>mine</td></tr><tr><td>You</td><td>your _____</td><td>yours</td></tr><tr><td>He, she, it his_____, her_____, its___</td><td></td><td>his, hers, its</td></tr><tr><td>Us</td><td>our_____</td><td>ours</td></tr><tr><td>Them</td><td>their_____</td><td>theirs</td></tr></table>

Application (Why?):

We use possessive pronouns to replace possessive nouns and show ownership.
- Before the noun, the pronoun replaces the possessive noun.
- Independently, the pronoun replaces the possessive noun **and** the object.

Formulas & Examples

Before the noun

Old sentence: The neighbors' dogs bark every night.

Formula 1:   Possessive Pronoun + noun + verb + finisher.

New sentence: Their dogs bark every night.

Independently

Old sentence: Jessica's cat is the one with the gray stripes.

Formula 2:   Possessive Pronoun + verb + finisher.

New sentence: Hers is the one with the gray stripes.

Possessive Pronouns

*Notes

1. Both types of possessive pronouns can be placed before or after the verb. (Example: *The cat with the gray stripes is Jessica's pet.*) The Preview Chart shows simple placement and examples of both types of possessive pronouns.

2. On the working chart, generate possessive nouns and objects for the subjects. (Examples: Lucy's homework, the family's house, the city's streets) Then change the possessive nouns to possessive pronouns for the collaborative sentences. See example below.

Owner	Possessive Pronoun	belongings		Verb
-family's	-their	-home	(picture)	-to light up
-mother's	-her	-cooking		-to fill

Coordinating Conjunctions: and, or, but

Language Objective: We will produce complete sentences using coordinating conjunctions to join: • Subjects, • Objects, • Clauses.	**Parts of Speech:** *Conjunctions* **and:** joins *like* things **or:** shows choice **but:** connects *unlike* things

Application (Why?): We use the coordinating conjunctions *and, or,* and *but* to join words in sentences showing a specific relationship between the words.	

Formulas & Examples	

Connect Subjects

Subject 1 + | and/or/but not | + Subject 2 + verb + finisher.

Example

Cookies | and | chocolate cake will be served after dinner.

Connect Objects

Subject + verb + object 1 + | and/or/but not | + object 2 + finisher.

Example

I would like to eat chocolate cake | or | cookies for dessert.

Connect Clauses

Subject 1 + verb 1, + | and/or/but | + subject 2 verb 2.

Example

The cookies were good, | but | the chocolate cake was better.

Coordinating Conjunctions

*Notes

1. Coordinating Conjunctions differ from Subordinating Conjunctions in two main ways:

- Coordinating Conjunctions can connect words, phrases, or entire clauses. Subordinating Conjunctions can only connect clauses.

- Coordinating Conjunctions connect items of similar weight or importance. Subordinating Conjunctions connect a clause that is more important (the independent clause) to another clause (the dependent clause) that tells more about the independent clause.

Comparative Adjectives

Compare two nouns.

Language Objective: We will produce complete sentences using comparative adjectives.	**Parts of Speech:** *Adjectives* *(of what kind)* **adjective(er)** OR **more + adjective** *(two syllables or less)* *(more than two syllables)* **Irregular:** good ⟶ better, bad ⟶ worse some/many ⟶ more, little ⟶ less

Application (Why?):
We use comparative adjectives to compare **two** nouns.

Formulas & Examples

Formula 1

Noun 1 + "to be" verb + adjective(er) + than + noun 2 + finisher.

Example

Oranges are sweeter than lemons.

Formula 2

Noun 1 + "to be" verb + more + adjective + than + noun 2 + finisher.

Example

A granola bar is a more nutritious snack than a candy bar.

Comparative Adjectives

*Notes

1. The syllable rule for more vs. –er is a *general* rule to which there are exceptions (i.e. "fun" becomes "more fun").

2. Comparative adjectives can be placed before the noun or as the complement of a linking verb. The above formulas focus on only comparing the two nouns. For advanced use, have students use comparative adjectives before nouns in any position of the sentence.

3. The following working chart setup can help students to follow the formulas.

Noun 1	To be Verb	Adjective	Noun 2
- Oranges		-sweet	-lemons
- Citrus fruits	(picture)	-healthy	-candy

Superlative Adjectives

Compare more than two nouns.

| **Language Objective:**
We will produce complete sentences using superlative adjectives. | **Parts of Speech:**

Adjectives
(of what kind)

adjective(est) OR **most + adjective**
(two syllables or less) *(more than two syllables)*

Irregular: good ⟶ best, bad ⟶ worst
some/many ⟶ most, little ⟶ least |

Application (Why?):
We use superlative adjectives to compare **more than two** nouns.

Formulas & Examples

Formula 1
Noun + "to be" verb + (the) + adjective(est) + of all _____ (group of nouns).

Example
Samantha was (the) tallest of all the students in her class.

Formula 2
Noun + "to be" verb + (the) + most + adjective + of all _____ (group of nouns).

Example
In Arizona, July and August are (the) most humid of all the months.

Superlative Adjectives

*Notes

1. The syllable rule for most vs. –est is a *general* rule to which there are exceptions (i.e. "fun" becomes "most fun").

2. Superlative adjectives can be placed before the noun or as the complement of a linking verb. The above formulas focus on only comparing more than two nouns.   For advanced use, have students use superlative adjectives before nouns in any position of the sentence.

3. The following working chart setup can help students to follow the formulas.

Noun	To be Verb	Adjective	"of all"
- Twin Towers		-tall	-American buildings
- Mt. Whitney	(picture)	-high	-California mountains

Adverbs of Manner

How?

Language Objective:	Parts of Speech:
We will produce complete sentences using adverbs of manner to describe the verb, in three positions: -before the verb -after the verb -at the beginning of the sentence.	*Adverb + Verb* How? (almost always end in **–ly**)

Application (Why?):
We use adverbs of manner to tell us *how* the verb is done.

Formulas & Examples

Formula 1

Subject + adverb + verb + finisher.

Example

Butterflies quickly dry their wings when they first emerge from their cocoons.

Formula 2

Subject + verb + adverb + finisher.

Example

Bees attack aggressively when threatened.

Formula 3

Adverb + subject + verb + finisher.

Example

Patiently, the spider waits for its prey to land on the web.

Adverbs of Manner

*Notes

1. Generate adverbs of manner after generating verbs on the working chart. See the example below.

Subject		Verb	How?
-herbivores		-to wander	-slowly
-Triceratops		-to graze	-patiently
-Tyrannosaurus Rex	(picture)	-to pursue	-aggressively
-carnivores		-to search	-desperately

Demonstrative Pronouns/Adjectives

Which one?

Language Objective:
We will write complete sentences using demonstrative pronouns and adjectives in the subject of the sentence.

Parts of Speech:

	Pronouns	Adjectives
Singular:		
(close)	This	This __(noun)___
(far)	That	That __(noun)___
Plural:		
(close)	These	These __(noun)__
(far)	Those	Those __(noun)__

Application (Why?):
We use demonstrative pronouns and adjectives to indicate which item we are talking about.

Formulas & Examples

Pronoun Formula

Demonstrative pronoun + verb +finisher.

Example

These are the best desserts I have ever tasted.

Adjective Formula

Demonstrative adjective + <u>noun</u> + verb + finisher.

Example

That muffin tastes even better than the one from yesterday.

Demonstrative Pronouns/Adjectives

*Notes

1. Demonstratives are not limited to the subject of the sentence. As an extension, have students replace subjects consisting of demonstrative adjectives and nouns with simply the demonstrative pronoun.

Example:

This sweater feels warm and comfortable. ⟶ This feels warm and comfortable.

2. Consider the following setup to facilitate the study.

Which one?	Subjects		Verb
-These	-delicacies		-to taste
-That	-display	(picture)	-to attract (customers)

Advanced Verb Tense Studies

- Command Verbs
- Modals: should, would, could
- Past Perfect
- Future Perfect
- Present Perfect Progressive
- Past Perfect Progressive
- Future Perfect Progressive
- Gerunds
- Passive Voice
- Conditional 1 (Real)
- Conditional 2 (Unreal)

Command Verbs

Language Objective:	Parts of Speech:
We will write complete sentences using command verbs to give directions to "you" in two forms: -declarative, -negative.	*Verbs* 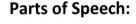 **You:** **base verb** (Modal) **do** 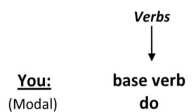

Application (Why?):

When we give a command, we are speaking directly to the person we are commanding so we are always talking to "you." Since we are always talking to "you," we don't have to say "you." Instead we start our sentence with a verb or with "please" if we want to be polite.

Formulas & Examples

Declarative

(You) + | base verb | + finisher.

Example

| Come | home immediately after the bell rings.

Negative

(You) + | do | + (not) + | base verb | + finisher.

Example

| Do | (not) | run | with the scissors <u>please</u>.

Command Verbs

*Notes

1. In command (imperative) sentence, the subject is the implied "you" meaning that the subject isn't actually stated.

2. Sentences using command verbs present an opportunity to use adverbs of time and direction. Example: Go _____ (now, later, home, outside, etc.).

3. The following setup of the working chart can help students to follow the formula.

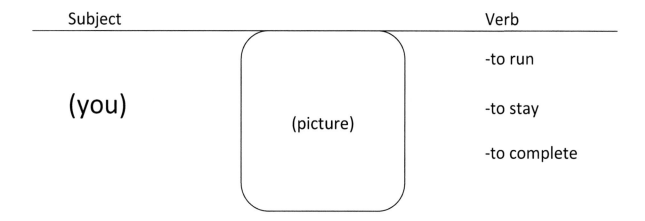

Subject		Verb
(you)	(picture)	-to run
		-to stay
		-to complete

Modals: should, would, could

<table>
<tr>
<td>

Language Objective:

We will write complete sentences using the modals should, would, and could in three forms:

-declarative,

-negative,

-interrogative.

</td>
<td>

Parts of Speech:

Verbs ➝ *Modals*

Should: shows obligation
Would: shows routine in past
Could: shows ability in past

modal + verb

</td>
</tr>
</table>

Application (Why?):
We use modals before the verb to add a very specific meaning to the verb.

Formulas & Examples

Declarative

Subject + modal + verb + finisher.

Example

In order to keep dry, she should wear a raincoat while she walks to work.

Negative

Subject + modal + not + verb + finisher.

Example

Her umbrella would not open all morning.

Interrogative

Modal + subject + verb + finisher?

Example

Could she drive to work instead of walking during last week's storm?

Modals

Should, Would, Could

*Notes

1. Should, would, and could, or the "rhyming" modals have specific meanings. Both "would" and "could" can be used to indicate the conditional, but can also be used to indicate past ability or routine, as shown in this preview chart. Have students start with the uses of "would" and "could" in the past before introducing their conditional uses.

2. Modals can be used in more forms than the simple "modal + verb" listed on the preview chart. They can be used in the following structures:

- modal + base verb

- modal + have + past participle

- modal + be + verb-ing

- modal + have + past participle + verb-ing

Past Perfect

Language Objective: We will write complete sentences in the past perfect verb tense in three forms: -declarative, -negative, -interrogative.	**Parts of Speech:** *Verbs* had + past participle

Application (Why?):
We use the past perfect to show:
- two actions that happened in the past,
- the first action was complete before the second began.

Formulas & Examples

Declarative

Subject + had + past participle + finisher.

Example

My family had finished dinner by the time I sat down at the table.

Negative

Subject + had + not + past participle + finisher.

Example

When the check arrived, we had not yet ordered dessert.

Interrogative

Had + subject + past participle + finisher?

Example

Had the waitress taken your order before she set the water on the table?

Past Perfect

*Notes

1. This tense utilizes a second event to illustrate a very specific time in the first event. Past Perfect is used to show two events in the past. The one that uses the Past Perfect construction was complete before the second event began.

2. The second event does not have to be explicitly stated in the sentence. It can be implied or it could have been presented previously in the text.

3. The time markers listed below can be used to introduce the second event. The first event must be conjugated into the Past Perfect. The second event is either conjugated in the simple past OR can simply be a prepositional phrase.

Example:

The leaves had fallen from the tree by the time winter arrived.

OR

The leaves had fallen from the tree by winter.

Past Perfect Time Markers

- By the time _____

- By _____

- Before _____

- When _____

- Already

Future Perfect

Language Objective: We will write complete sentences in the future perfect verb tense in three forms: -declarative, -negative, -interrogative.	**Parts of Speech:** *Verbs* 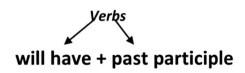 **will have + past participle**

Application (Why?):
We use the future perfect to show:
- two actions that will happen in the future,
- the first action will be complete before the second begins.

Formulas & Examples

Declarative

Subject + will have + past participle + finisher.

Example

In 2011, we will have consumed half of the producible oil on the planet.

Negative

Subject + will + not + have + past participle + finisher.

Example

Thousands of sea turtle eggs will not have hatched by the time the mother returns to the ocean.

Interrogative

Will + subject + have + past participle + finisher?

Example

Will the seasonal flowers have bloomed before the Spring ends?

Future Perfect

*Notes

1. This tense utilizes a second event to illustrate a very specific time in the first event. Future perfect is used to show two events in the future. The one that uses the Future Perfect construction will be complete before the second event begins.

2. The second event does not have to be explicitly stated in the sentence. It can be implied or it could have been presented previously in the text.

3. The following time markers can be used to introduce the second event. The first event must be conjugated into the Future Perfect. The second event is either conjugated in the Simple Present OR can simply be a prepositional phrase.

Example:

The leaves will have fallen from the trees by the time winter arrives.

OR

The leave will have fallen from the trees by winter.

Future Perfect Time Markers

- By the time _____

- By _____

- Before _____

- When _____

- Already

- In/On _____

Present Perfect Progressive

Language Objective:	Parts of Speech:
We will write complete sentences in the present perfect progressive verb tense in three forms: -declarative, -negative, -interrogative.	*Verbs* **has/have + been + verb(ing)** singular subject- **has** plural subject- **have** (I/you)

Application (Why?):
We use the present perfect progressive to show actions that:
- started in the past,
- ended recently or continue in the present,
- have been ongoing.

Formulas & Examples

Declarative

<u>Subject</u> + has/have + been + verb(ing) + finisher.

Example

<u>The gubernatorial candidates</u> have been debating their positions on the financial crisis <u>for the last twenty minutes.</u>

Negative

<u>Subject</u> + has/have + <u>not</u> + been + verb(ing) + finisher.

Example

<u>As the attacks become more personal, the</u> <u>moderator</u> has not been addressing the key issues.

Interrogative

Has/Have + <u>subject</u> + been + verb(ing) + finisher?

Example

Have <u>the audience members</u> been forming <u>their decisions about which candidate they prefer</u> during the debate?

Present Perfect Progressive

*Notes

1. This tense is used to illustrate an ongoing event that was recently completed, or started in the past and continues in the present.

2. Time markers are helpful for all of the perfect progressive tenses. Try using the examples below.

Perfect Progressive Time Markers

Try adding these to your sentences to provide more detail.

Past	Present	Future
• since	• since	• since
• for	• for	• for
• before	• during	• before
• when	• recently	• when
• by the time	• lately	• by the time
• finally	• as of late	• finally

Past Perfect Progressive

Language Objective: We will write complete sentences in the past perfect progressive verb tense in three forms: -declarative, -negative, -interrogative.	**Parts of Speech:** *Verbs* **had + been + verb(ing)**

Application (Why?):
We use the past perfect progressive to show:
- two actions that happened in the past,
- the first action was ongoing and
- recently completed when the second action began.

Formulas & Examples

Declarative

Subject + had + been + verbing + finisher.

Example

Relief agencies had been hurriedly delivering medical supplies when the first aftershock struck.

Negative

Subject + had + not + been + verbing + finisher.

Example

Volunteers had not been searching for survivors for very long by the time the building collapsed.

Interrogative

Had + subject + been + verbing + finisher?

Example

Had refuges been arriving in Port-au-Prince for many days before they found shelter?

Future Perfect Progressive

Language Objective:	Parts of Speech:
We will write complete sentences in the future perfect progressive verb tense in three forms: -declarative, -negative, -interrogative.	*Verbs* 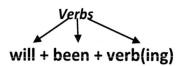 **will + been + verb(ing)**

Application (Why?):
We use the future perfect progressive to show:
- two actions that will happen in the future,
- the first action will be ongoing and
- will be recently completed when the second action begins.

Formulas & Examples

Declarative

Subject + will have + been + verbing + finisher.

Example

The sprinklers will have been running for three hours by the time they turn off.

Negative

Subject + will + not + have + been + verbing + finisher.

Example

Jack and Sarah will not have been rehearsing their lines for very long when drama class ends.

Interrogative

Will + subject + have + been + verbing + finisher?

Example

Will the hikers have been walking for miles by the time they find the trail?

Gerunds

Language Objective: We will write complete sentences using gerunds as the: -subject of the sentence, -subject complement of the sentence.	**Parts of Speech:** *Gerunds* ↓ **Verb-ing** acting like a noun

Application (Why?):
Gerunds allow us to use verbs as nouns in sentences by adding –ing.

Formulas & Examples

Subject

Gerund + to be verb + finisher.

Example

Jogging is my favorite way to relieve stress.

Subject Complement

Subject + to be verb + gerund + finisher.

Example

The toddler's least favorite activity is napping.

Gerunds

*Notes

1. Because gerunds take the place of nouns, they can go in any position that a noun can, including direct objects and objects of the preposition, which are not shown on this preview chart.

2. Gerunds as subject complements look exactly like verbs in the progressive form. Students need to understand that the "to be verb" is equating the gerund to the subject rather than showing an action done by the subject.

Example:

Susan is running a race. (The subject, Susan, is doing the action of "running.")

vs.

Tomorrow's challenge will be running a race.

(The subject, tomorrow's challenge, is **not** doing the action of running. Rather the subject and the complement are the same. Tomorrow's challenge = running a race. Running=gerund.)

*Quick test: If the word ending in –ing can be replaced with "the act/activity of_____," it's probably a gerund. In the examples above, "Susan is 'the activity of' running a race." does not work, but "Tomorrow's challenge will be 'the activity of running a race.'" does.

3. The following setup for a working chart will help students see the gerund and subject complement relationship.

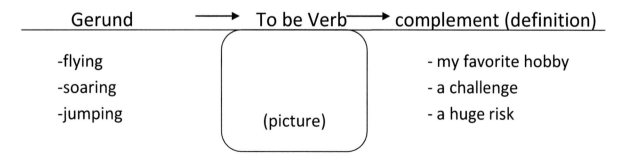

Gerund	⟶ To be Verb ⟶	complement (definition)
-flying		- my favorite hobby
-soaring		- a challenge
-jumping	(picture)	- a huge risk

Passive Voice

Language Objective: We will write complete sentences in the passive voice in three forms: -declarative, -negative, -interrogative.	**Parts of Speech:** *Verbs* **Subject** + To be verb + past participle (was object) *Simple tenses:* was, were/ am, is, are/ will be *Progressive tenses:* (was, were/am, is, are/will be) **+ being** *Perfect tenses:* had/has, have/will have **+ been** *Perfect Progressive tenses:* had/has, have/will have **+ been being**

Application (Why?):

We use the passive voice to hide the actor in the sentence. We do this by changing the object of the sentence to the subject of the sentence, which allows us to focus on the item receiving the action rather than the person or thing doing the action.

Formulas & Examples

Declarative	<u>Subject</u> + to be verb + past participle + finisher. (was object)
Example	<u>Old sentence:</u> Sam threw the pencil at his teacher. <u>New sentence:</u> The pencil was thrown at the teacher.
Negative	<u>Subject</u> + to be verb + not + past participle + finisher. (was object)
Example	<u>Grades</u> were not submitted on time by the faculty this semester.
Interrogative	To be verb + <u>subject</u> + past participle + finisher? (was object)
Example	Was the book returned to the library before the due date?

Passive Voice

*Notes

1. The passive voice can be used in any tense, but all examples use the simple past.

2. In the passive voice, the object of an active voice sentence becomes the subject of the new sentence. Because of this students will have to generate transitive verbs. A transitive verb is a verb that requires an object.

Example: The verb "to throw" usually requires an object to say what was thrown.

The verb "to stand," however, does not take an object.

3. Due to the complexity of this tense, students should first produce active sentences and then convert them to passive sentences before moving directly to passive sentences.

4. The following setup of a working chart will show students how the objects of active voice sentence become the subjects of passive voice sentences.

*Write the objects on a separate sheet of paper and then physically move them to cover the original subjects in order to create a passive voice sentence.

Subject	To be Verb	Verb	Object
- shortstop		-to catch	-the line drive
- professional athlete		-to celebrate	- the victory
- winning team	(picture)	-to throw	- the 90 mph pitch
- umpire		-to call	- the strike

Conditional 1 (real)

Language Objective: We will write complete sentences in the conditional in three forms: -Present Real -Past Real -Future Real.	Parts of Speech: *If/When + clause, + clause.* **When:** used if something happens regularly **If:** less likely to happen *If/When clause introduces condition. The other clause shows the certain result.

Application (Why?):
We use the conditional in the "real" forms to show certain results when one condition is met.

Formulas & Examples

Present Real

If/When + clause in simple present, + (then) + clause in simple present.

Example

When the puppy greets her at the door, the little girl smiles.

Past Real

If/When + clause in simple past, + clause in simple past.

Example

If it rained, we stayed inside and played board games.

Future Real

If/When + clause in simple present, clause in simple future.

Example

When she hears the timer go off, she will take the cookies out of the oven.

*Notes: The clauses can be flipped.

Example 1 could also be: "The little girl smiles when the puppy greets her at the door."

Conditional (real)

*Notes

1. The real conditional is used to indicate certain results when a condition is met.

2. The conditional construction requires two clauses. The clause that begins with the "if" or "when" introduces the condition. The other clause introduces the result.

3. The conditional real in the present tense is used to show anticipated results from the condition. Example: If it's windy, I wear a scarf.

4. The conditional real in the past is used to show regular actions based on met conditions in the past. Example: When it was nap time in kindergarten, we would pretend to be sleeping.

5. The conditional real in the future is used to show certain results based on a condition that has not yet been met, but will be or might be in the future. Example: If that candidate wins the election, the incumbent president will return to his home state.

6. To assist students in understanding the conditional, consider using the graphic below.

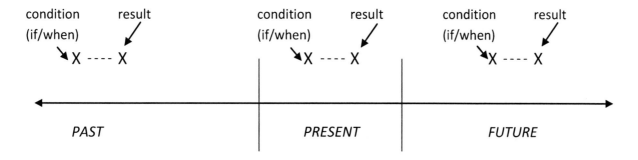

Conditional 2 (unreal)

Language Objective:	Parts of Speech:
We will write complete sentences in the conditional in three forms: -Present Unreal -Past Unreal -Future Unreal.	*If + clause, + clause.* *If clause introduces the unreal condition. The other clause shows the imagined result.

Application (Why?):

We use the conditional in the "unreal" forms to show imagined results based on an untrue condition.

Formulas & Examples

Present Real

If + clause in simple past, + (then) + subject + would + verb + finisher.

Example

If she studied more, she would pass the test.

Past Real

If + clause in past perfect, + subject + would have + verb + finisher..

Example

If we had not missed the bus, we would have arrived to school on time.

Future Real

If + subject + were + going to + verb, + subject + would + be + verb-ing + finisher.

Example

If I were going to stay late after school, I would be making arrangements for another ride home.

*Notes: The clauses can be flipped.

Example 1 could also be: "She would pass the test, if she studied more."

Conditional (unreal)

*Notes

1. The real conditional is used to indicate possible results from a condition that has *not* been met.

2. The conditional construction requires two clauses. The clause that begins with the "if" introduces the condition. The other clause introduces the imagined result.

3. The conditional unreal in the present is used to show possible results from changing a current situation. Example: If we lived closer, we would see each other more often.

4. The conditional unreal in the past is used to show possible results by changing an action that has *already* happened. This sentence structure requires the past perfect construction (with a modal in the result clause). Example: We would never have accepted the money if we had known it was counterfeit.

5. The conditional unreal in the future is used to show a possible result from a condition in the future that might not be met. The condition clause uses the past tense to be verb, "were" while the result clause requires a past tense modal. Example: If money were limitless, we would be going on an African safari for our vacation instead of taking a road trip to the coast.

6. To assist students in understanding the conditional, consider using the graphic below.

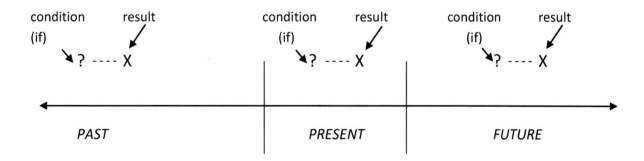

Advanced Grammar Studies

- Adverbs of Frequency
- Subordinating Conjunctions of Cause
- Adverbs of Direction
- Adverbs of Time
- Adverbs of Degree
- Reflexive Pronouns
- Indefinite Pronouns
- Appositives
- Comparative Adverbs
- Superlative Adverbs
- Correlative Conjunctions
- Subordinating Conjunctions of Contrast
- Subordinating Conjunctions of Time
- Subordinating Conjunctions of Condition

Adverbs of Frequency

How often?

	Parts of Speech:
Language Objective: We will produce complete sentences using adverbs of frequency to describe the verb or adjective.	*Adverb + Verb* 100% 0% **Always**---------- **Sometimes**-----------**Never** Often Occasionally Frequently Rarely Usually Seldom Regularly Hardly ever

Application (Why?):
We use adverbs of frequency to tell us *how often* the verb is done.

Formulas & Examples

Formula 1

Subject + adverb + <u>verb</u> + finisher.

Example

Migrating whales rarely <u>travel</u> away from their pods.

Formula 2

Subject + verb + adverb   +   finisher.

Example

Tourists <u>have</u> seldom <u>seen</u> the elusive jaguar in its natural habitat.

Formula 3

Adverb + subject + <u>verb</u> + finisher.

Example

Occasionally, wild animals <u>wander</u> into city centers.

Adverbs of Frequency

*Notes

1. Not all of the adverbs can be used in each position. Occasionally, frequently, usually, often and sometimes can go at the beginning. (Formula 3)

2. Unlike other types of adverbs, adverbs of frequency do not go after all verbs. They can only go in the middle of the verb phrase (See Example 2), as used in perfect tenses and the passive voice.

3. Use the following setup for the working chart to show students the relationship between the verb and the adverb.

Subject		Verb	How often?
-the tides		-to rise	-always
- waves	(picture)	-to crash	-usually
- currents		-to flow uphill	-never

Subordinating Conjunctions of Cause

Why?

Parts of Speech:

Conjunctions
(subordinating)

Language Objective:
We will write complete sentences using subordinating conjunctions of cause to connect two clauses.

Clause= subject + verb ⟶ Clause + conjunction + clause
Because: introduces reason/cause (newer information)
So that: introduces effect
Since: introduces reason/cause (old information)

Application (Why?):

We use subordinating conjunctions of cause to connect two clauses (ideas) showing:
- why, or a cause/effect relationship.
- The clause that begins with the subordinating conjunction tells us something about the other clause.

Formulas & Examples

Formula 1	Clause 1 + subordinating conjunction + clause 2.
Example	At noon, the bell rang so that the students could go to lunch.
Formula 2	Subordinating conjunction + clause 1, clause 2
Example	Since you didn't turn in your homework, you won't be going to break.

Subordinating Conjunctions of Cause

*Notes

1. Show students that clauses are linked by the subordinating conjunction. The independent clause can stand alone as a sentence. The clause introduced by the conjunction tells something more about the independent clause and cannot stand alone as a sentence. In this case, it tells "why."

2. Consider the following setup for the working chart.

Subject		Verb	Why?
-clouds		-to gather	-because...
-winds	(picture)	-to howl	-since...
-residents		-to take cover	-so that...

Adverbs of Direction

Where?

Language Objective: We will produce complete sentences using adverbs of direction after the verb.	Parts of Speech:
	Adverb + Verb
	Where?

Application (Why?):
We use adverbs of direction to tell us **where** the verb is done.

Formulas & Examples

Formula	Subject + <u>verb</u> + adverb + finisher.
Example 1	Please take the dog outside.
Example 2	After the laundry is folded, I carry it upstairs.
Example 3	At the whistle, the runners sprint forward.

*Notes:

1. Use the same working chart setup as presented for Adverbs of Manner and Adverbs of Frequency. Instead of asking "How?" or "How Often?"ask "Where?."

Adverbs of Time

When?

Language Objective:
We will produce complete sentences using adverbs of manner to describe the verb, in three positions:
-before the verb
-after the verb
-at the beginning of the sentence.

Parts of Speech:

Adverb + Verb

(Past)	(Present)	(Future)
yesterday	today	tomorrow
already lately currently soon		
earlier recently presently		next

Application (Why?):
We use adverbs of manner to tell us *when* the verb is done.

Formulas & Examples

Formula 1	Subject + adverb + <u>verb</u> + finisher.
Example	The moon <u>is</u> currently <u>orbiting</u> around the earth.
Formula 2	Subject + <u>verb</u> + adverb + finisher.
Example	The moon <u>will enter</u> its fourth phase tomorrow.
Formula 3	Adverb + subject + <u>verb</u> + finisher.
Example	Lately, the clouds <u>have been blocking</u> the sun.

*Notes:

1. Use the same working chart setup as presented for Adverbs of Manner and Adverbs of Frequency. Instead of asking "How?" or "How Often?" ask "When?."

Adverbs of Degree

How much?

Language Objective:	**Parts of Speech:**
We will produce complete sentences using adverbs of degree to describe the verb, in one position: -before the verb.	*Adverb + Verb* (0%) ←———————————————→ (100%) hardly almost really completely slightly highly extremely partially moderately strongly totally adequately very entirely

Application (Why?):
We use adverbs of degree to tell us *how much* about the verb.

Formulas & Examples

Formula

Subject + adverb + <u>verb</u> + finisher.

Example 1

The lion cub slightly <u>wounded</u> the gazelle with its dull claws and small teeth.

Example 2

The small elephant almost <u>escaped</u> the crocodile's attack.

Example 3

The passing storm completely <u>destroyed</u> the makeshift tents.

*Notes:

1. Use the same working chart setup as presented for Adverbs of Manner and Adverbs of Frequency. Instead of asking "How?" or "How Often?" ask "How much?"

Indefinite Pronouns

Not sure? Use an indefinite pronoun!

Language Objective:
We will write complete sentences using singular and plural indefinite pronouns as the subject of the sentence.

Parts of Speech:

Pronouns
Indefinite Pronouns

Singular			Plural
everybody	everyone	everything	few
somebody	someone	something	some
anybody	anyone	anything	others
nobody	no one	nothing	many
			several
another other each		either one	both

Application (Why?):
We use indefinite pronouns when we don't know the exact number, person, or thing that the pronoun will be replacing.

Formulas & Examples

Singular Formula

| Singular indefinite pronoun | + to be verb + finisher.

Example

| Everyone | is welcome to attend the Thanksgiving feast at the church.

Plural Formula

| Plural indefinite pronoun | + to be verb + finisher.

Example

Although many parishioners travel on Thanksgiving, | several | were at the luncheon.

*Notes: Indefinite pronouns are not limited to the subject of the sentence. They can also be used in any position that a noun can be used.

Reflexive Pronouns

Language Objective:	Parts of Speech:
We will write complete sentences using reflexive pronouns after the verb.	**Pronouns**

Parts of Speech:

Pronouns

Subject (before the verb)	**Reflexive** (after the verb)
I	myself
you	yourself
he	himself
she	herself
it	itself
we	ourselves
you	yourselves
they	themselves

Application (Why?):

We use reflexive pronouns to show that the person receiving the action is the same as the person doing the action. Reflexive pronouns must always match the subject of the sentence. Reflexive pronouns are either the direct or indirect object of the sentence.

Formulas & Examples

Formula

Subject + verb + finisher (with reflexive pronoun).

Example 1

Melissa and Shannon taught themselves to read Egyptian hieroglyphics.

Example 2

For her birthday, she bought herself a new wardrobe.

Example 3

My new cellphone updates itself every time I turn it on.

Reflexive Pronouns

*Notes

1. For this *Grammar Study*, students will have to generate verbs that the subjects can do to themselves. The following working chart setup facilitates this construction.

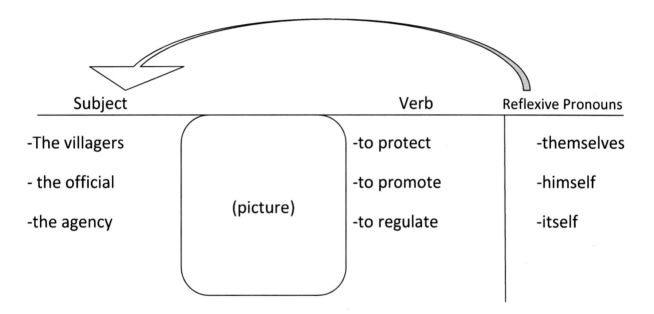

Subject		Verb	Reflexive Pronouns
-The villagers		-to protect	-themselves
- the official	(picture)	-to promote	-himself
-the agency		-to regulate	-itself

Appositives

Define a noun.

Language Objective:
We will write complete sentences using appositives in two locations:
-after the subject,
-after the object.

Parts of Speech:

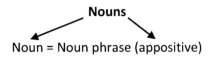

Nouns

Noun = Noun phrase (appositive)

Application (Why?):
We use appositives to define or re-name the noun directly before or after referring to the noun. Appositives provide clarity or further definition for the noun. They are able to directly replace the noun.

Formulas & Examples

Formula 1

Subject, + appositive, + verb + finisher.

Example

Rhode Island, the smallest state in the United States, was one of the original thirteen colonies.

Formula 2

Subject + verb + object, + appositive.

Example

The first U.S. President was George Washington, the Commander-in-Chief of the Continental Army.

Appositives

*Notes

1. For this *Grammar Study*, students will have to generate appositives, or other definitions, for the subjects. The following working chart setup facilitates this construction.

2. Remind students that the appositives they generate must be *nouns* and must be able to *replace the subject*.

Subjects	Appositives		Verbs
- the President	- a former Senator from Illinois		-to address
-the First Lady	-an advocate for national nutrition	(picture)	-to endorse
-the Secret Service agents	-the President's personal guards		-to survey

Comparative Adverbs

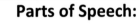

Compare two verbs.

Language Objective:	Parts of Speech:
We will produce complete sentences using comparative adverbs in two forms: -add –er to the end - add "more" to the beginning	*Adverbs* 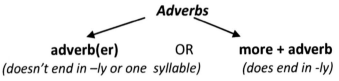 **adverb(er)**　　OR　　**more + adverb** *(doesn't end in –ly or one syllable)*　*(does end in -ly)* **Irregular:** well ⟶ better, badly ⟶ worse little ⟶ less　　　far ⟶ farther

Application (Why?):
We use comparative adverbs to compare **two** verbs.

Formulas & Examples

Formula 1

Subject + <u>verb</u> + adverb-er + than + finisher.

Example

We <u>learn</u> formulas faster in algebra than we <u>learned</u> them in geometry.

Formula 2

Subject + <u>verb</u> + more + adverb + than + finisher.

Example

However, our teacher <u>assesses</u> us more frequently this semester than during the last one.

Comparative Adverbs

*Notes

1. "Than" is not needed in the sentence construction, but helps to clarify that two verbs or adjectives are being compared.

2. Comparative adverbs can also be used to compare adjectives. Example: Her shoes are a brighter red than mine.

3. Very few adverbs will fall under the first formula, that of adding –er, as most adverbs end in –ly already.

4. On the working chart, students will have to generate verbs that can be done by both subjects of the sentence (For example, the verb "to fly" will not work with the subjects "bird" and "elephant.")

5. The following working chart setup can help students to follow the formulas.

Subject	To be Verb	Verb	adverb
- cheetahs		-to run	-faster
- tortoises	(picture)	-to live	-longer

Superlative Adverbs

Compare **more than two** verbs.

Language Objective:	Parts of Speech:
We will produce complete sentences using superlative adverbs in two forms: -add –est to the end - add "most" to the beginning	*Adverbs* **adverb(est)** OR **most + adverb** *(doesn't end in –ly or one syllable)* *(does end in -ly)* **Irregular:** well ⟶ best, badly ⟶ worst little ⟶ least far ⟶ farthest

Application (Why?):
We use superlative adverbs to compare **more than two** verbs.

Formulas & Examples

Formula 1

Subject + <u>verb</u> + the + | adverb-est | + of all/in all +finisher.

Example

Flight 279 <u>arrives</u> the | latest | of all the incoming planes at this airport.

Formula 2

Subject + <u>verb</u> +the + | most + adverb | + of all/in all + finisher.

Example

Those baggage handlers <u>carry</u> the luggage the | most carefully | of all the workers.

Superlative Adverbs

*Notes

1. "Of all/In all" is not needed in the sentence construction, but helps to clarify that more than two verbs or adjectives are being compared.

Consider showing students that they are selecting a specific person or item from a larger group. For example, the sentence "The gold medalist swims the fastest of all the competitors in the Olympics." could be illustrated as:

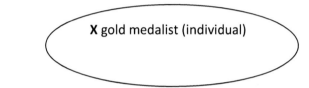

X gold medalist (individual)

Competitors in the Olympics (name for whole group)

2. Superlative adverbs can also be used to compare adjectives. Example: Her shoes are the brightest red of all the shoes I have ever seen.

3. The following working chart setup can help students to follow the formulas.

Subject	To be Verb	Verb	adverb	of all_____
- cheetahs		-to run	-fastest	-land mammals
- tortoises	(picture)	-to live	-longest	-reptiles

Correlative Conjunctions

<table>
<tr>
<td>

Language Objective:
We will produce complete sentences using correlative conjunctions to join:
- Subjects,
- Objects,
- Verbs.

</td>
<td>

Parts of Speech:
Conjunctions
(correlative)

either.... or – choice between two
neither...nor – both are negative
not only... but also- both are positive

</td>
</tr>
</table>

Application (Why?):
We use correlative conjunctions in pairs to show relationships between parallel, or similar items.

Formulas & Examples

Connect Subjects

Correlative conjunction + subject 1 + correlative conjunction + subject 2 + verb + finisher.

Example

Either hail or snow will fall tonight.

Connect Objects

Subject + verb + correlative conjunction + object 1 + correlative conjunction + object 2 + finisher.

Example

In the morning, you will find not only frost, but also icicles on your car.

Connect Clauses

Subject + correlative conjunction + verb 1 + correlative conjunction + verb 2 + finisher.

Example

Being from Southern California, I have neither seen nor touched snow.

Conjunctions of Contrast

Difference

Language Objective:
We will write complete sentences using subordinating conjunctions of contrast to connect two clauses.

Parts of Speech:

Conjunctions
(subordinating)

Clause= subject + verb ⟶ Clause + conjunction + clause
but: two unlike items
whereas: unlike but parallel items
although, though, even though: contrary result

Application (Why?):
We use subordinating conjunctions of contrast to connect two clauses (ideas) showing:
- a contrastive relationship.
- The clause that begins with the subordinating conjunction gives us information about the difference from the independent clause.

Formulas & Examples

Formula 1

Clause 1 + subordinating conjunction + clause 2.

Example

My sister's dog runs with her every day whereas mine prefers to nap indoors.

("Whereas" could be replaced with "but." "Whereas" was used to show parallel situations: what two dogs like to do.)

Formula 2

Subordinating conjunction + clause 1, clause 2

Example

Even though my dog was tired, she still exercised with me.

("Although" was used because one would expect a different outcome, or contrary result based on the information.)

*Notes:

1. The conjunction "but" can be used to replace the other conjunctions listed in all situations. The other conjunctions, however, are used to provide more specific information about the contrasting ideas, and are *not* interchangeable.

Subordinating Conjunctions of Time

When?

Language Objective: We will write complete sentences using subordinating conjunctions of time to connect two clauses.	**Parts of Speech:** ***Conjunctions*** *(subordinating)* Clause= subject + verb ⟶ Clause + conjunction + clause **after:** introduces first action **before:** introduces second action **since:** introduces first action **while:** introduces actions from same time **as:** introduces actions from same time

Application (Why?):

We use subordinating conjunctions of time to connect two clauses (ideas) showing:
- a time or sequence relationship.
- The clause that begins with the subordinating conjunction gives us information about the time of the independent clause.

Formulas & Examples

Formula 1

Clause 1 + | subordinating conjunction | + clause 2.

Example

She drank her soda | while | she watched her siblings play.

Formula 2

| Subordinating conjunction | + clause 1, clause 2

Example

| Since | he left high school, the student has learned two new languages.

*Notes:

1. Show students that clauses are linked by the subordinating conjunction. The independent clause can stand alone as a sentence. The clause introduced by the conjunction tells something more about the independent clause and cannot stand alone as a sentence. In this case, it tells "when."

2. Since and after are <u>not</u> interchangeable. The second example, when replaced with "after" becomes, "After he left high school, the students *learned* two new languages."

Subordinating Conjunctions of Condition

It will happen when....

Language Objective:	Parts of Speech:
We will write complete sentences using subordinating conjunctions of condition to connect two clauses.	**Conjunctions** *(subordinating)* Clause= subject + verb ⟶ Clause + conjunction + clause **if:** Independent clause will happen based on dependent. **unless:** introduces exceptions **as soon as:** once something else happens

Application (Why?):
We use subordinating conjunctions of condition to connect two clauses (ideas) showing:
- a dependent relationship.
- The clause that begins with the subordinating conjunction gives us information about the circumstances under which the other clause can happen.

Formulas & Examples

Formula 1

Clause 1 + subordinating conjunction + clause 2.

Example

Students will not be going on the field trip unless they return their permission slips.

Formula 2

Subordinating conjunction + clause 1, clause 2

Example

As soon as everyone's backpacks are packed, we will board the bus.

*Notes:

1. The conjunction "if" can be used interchangeably with "unless" and "as soon as" though it slightly changes the meaning. "Unless" and "As soon as" show a very specific relationship and *cannot* be used to replace each other.

Lists

Need some help thinking of words that fall into the specific parts of speech?
Throughout the subsequent pages you'll find examples of the main categories for each part of speech. These words are just a sampling, but can be used in *Grammar Studies, Verb Tense Studies,* and on the *Grammar Wall.*

- Adjectives

- Nouns

- Pronouns

- Verbs

- Adverbs

- Prepositions

- Conjunctions

- Interjections

- Parts of Speech Clues

- Basic Syntax Rules

Adjectives

Which one?		How many?	
Articles	*Demonstrative*	*Definite*	*Indefinite*
a	this	seven	many
an	that	twenty-six	several
the	these	900	few
	those	12.5	multitudes of
			all

What kind?
Observation/Quality

abnormal	healthy	neat	tedious
astute	honest	needy	terrible
average	humble	nosy	traumatic
beautiful	intelligent	obedient	unbelievable
benevolent	irrelevant	oppressive	understanding
brave	irregular	outrageous	unique
courteous	joyful	peaceful	valuable
courageous	jubilant	peculiar	vehement
clever	judgmental	powerful	voracious
daring	kept	quaint	weary
devious	kind	quick	wicked
doubtful	knowledgeable	quirky	worn
eccentric	laughable	radiant	yappy
elegant	loud	relevant	yielding
enduring	lucky	ridiculous	yummy
fancy	magnanimous	sassy	zany
finicky	magnificent	serious	zealous
furious	meticulous	studious	zestful
generous			
glorious			
graceful			

Size	Shape	Age	Color
colossal	round	ancient	burgundy
grandiose	straight	contemporary	crimson
miniscule	triangular	modern	magenta

Origin	Material	*Comparative*	*Superlative*
cosmopolitan	glass	more interesting	most ingenious
Japanese	plastic	lovelier	smarter
medieval	wooden		

Nouns

Common

person		place		thing		idea	
singular	plural	singular	plural	singular	plural	singular	plural
acrobat	artists	aviary	aviaries	appliance	apples	anxiety	adorations
busboy	butchers	beach	beaches	binder	bags	belief	beliefs
chief	captains	cove	coves	couch	chains	courage	choices
driver	divers	dell	dells	desk	dice	doubt	doubts
employee	employers	environment	environments	envelope	echoes	evil	emotions
firefighter	fugitives	forest	forests	fern	folders	fear	fears
grandfather	governors	grassland	grasslands	gem	geese	grace	grievances
helper	heirs	hearth	hearths	hip	hangers	hope	hopes
intern	immigrants	island	islands	ignition	indices	ignorance	impunities
jailer	jurors	jetty	jetties	jar	jellies	justice	joys
kinsman	keepers	kennel	kennels	kernel	kites	kindness	kindnesses
lieutenant	lawyers	lawn	lawns	log	ladders	luck	laws
manager	men	mountain	mountains	mask	mice	mercy	mercies
neighbor	natives	nursery	nurseries	nap	nuclei	neglect	negotiations
operator	owners	oasis	oases	octopus	oxen	ownership	obsessions
pianist	people	peninsula	peninsulas	penny	poles	peace	perplexities
queen	queens	quadrant	quadrants	quarrel	quilts	quiet	questions
rancher	referees	reef	reefs	ration	razors	resistance	religions
sailor	sergeants	shore	shores	shoulder	stamps	safety	sciences
teammate	thieves	town	towns	towel	trunks	trust	truths
umpire	ushers	university	universities	umbrella	unicycles	unity	ultimatums
vagabond	vagrants	village	villages	veil	verbs	veracity	values
watchman	wives	warehouse	warehouses	wing	wolves	wisdom	worries
youngster	yodelers	yard	yards	year	yelps	yearning	yearnings
zookeeper	zealots	zoo	zones	zenith	zippers	zeal	zoology

Proper

People	Places	Things	Ideas	Compound	Collective	Non-count	Gerunds
Mr. Jones	Utah	Liberty Bell	Christianity	backpack	team	air	running
Dr. Brown	China	Declaration of Independence	Confucianism	dishwasher	pod	sand	reading
Heidi	San Diego		English	lunchbox	crew	flour	swimming
Pres. Obama	Venus	Treaty of Versailles	Quantum Physics	racecar	council	water	knowing
Ivan	Indian Ocean			football	bunch	sugar	listening
				software	colony	furniture	trying

Pronouns

Personal Subject (before verb)	Personal Object (after verb)	Possessive (before noun)	(alone)	Reflexive
I	me	my	mine	myself
you	you	your	yours	yourself
he	him	his	his	himself
she	her	her	hers	herself
it	it	its	its	itself
we	us	our	ours	ourselves
they	them	their	theirs	themselves

Indefinite			Demonstrative	Reciprocal
person	*place*	*thing*		
no one	nowhere	nothing	this	each other
someone	somewhere	something	that	one another
anyone	anywhere	anything	these	
everyone	everywhere	everything	those	
nobody		none	Interrogative	Relative
somebody		all	who	that
anybody		several	what	which
everybody		few	where	
			when	
			why	
			how	

Verbs

Action

Physical

to accelerate	to navigate		
to balance	to ooze		
to catch	to puncture		
to drown	to quarry		
to extend	to raid		
to float	to surrender		
to gallop	to trample		
to hurl	to usurp		
to ignite	to vanish		
to jostle	to wander		
to kneel	to x-ray		
to launch	to yelp		
to maneuver	to zoom		

Mental

to acknowledge	to memorize
to believe	to negate
to concede	to oblige
to disagree	to perceive
to evaluate	to question
to forget	to remember
to generalize	to synthesize
to humble (oneself)	to theorize
to intend	to understand
to jeopardize	to validate
to know	to worry
to legitimize	to yearn

Linking

to be	to become
to seem	to grow
to appear	to see
to feel	to smell
to sound	to remain

Modals

can	do
have to	does
ought to	did
could	may
would	might
should	must
	shall

Phrasal

to sit up	to call off
to sit down	to calm down
to stand up	to catch up
to throw up	to check out
to blow up	to dress up
to break down	to hang on
to break up	to hang out
to get over	to show off
to warm up	to wake up

Irregular

to arise	to eat	to hold	to read
to awake	to fall	to keep	to run
to begin	to feel	to know	to see
to build	to fight	to lay	to sell
to buy	to find	to lead	to sing
to choose	to fly	to lose	to swim
to come	to get	to make	to take
to cut	to give	to meet	to teach
to do	to go	to pay	to think
to draw	to grow	to put	to wear
to dream	to hear	to quit	to write

Adverbs

Manner

accidentally	gracefully	mechanically	successfully
blindly	happily	nervously	triumphantly
cautiously	innocently	officially	unexpectedly
daringly	jealously	politely	viciously
efficiently	knowingly	quietly	well
ferociously	lovingly	respectfully	zealously

Direction	Time	Frequency	Degree
away	now	never	not
forward	soon	seldom	more
here	later	rarely	somewhat
there	today	sometimes	slightly
onward	tomorrow	occasionally	partly
upside-down	tonight	regularly	practically
backwards	yesterday	usually	really
abroad	earlier	frequently	very
apart	currently	constantly	quite
sideways	presently	often	increasingly
westward	lately	always	too
home	immediately	daily	so
inside	finally	monthly	totally
outside	next	weekly	extremely
nearby	recently	annually	completely

Conjunctive (transition words)

addition	emphasis	contrast	causation
also	certainly	however	accordingly
further	still	yet	as a result
furthermore	in fact	instead	consequently
in addition	indeed	nonetheless	thus
likewise	undoubtedly	nevertheless	hence
moreover		conversely	therefore
		otherwise	

Prepositions

Location		Time	Purpose
above	in	about	because of
across	in front of	after	by way of
adjacent to	inside	around	due to
after	into	at	for
against	next to	before	for the purpose of
alongside	of	between	for the sake of
amid	off	by	in order to
among	on	close to	out of
around	onto	during	owing to
at	opposite	for	
atop	out	from	
behind	over	in	
below	past	of	
beneath	through	past	
beside	throughout	prior to	
between	to	since	
beyond	under	subsequent to	
by	underneath	till	
for	upon	until	
from	within	within	

Preposition that tells how: by _____ (+ verb-ing)

Conjunctions

Coordinating

addition	reason	contrast	choice	Correlative
and	so for	but yet no	or	either…or neither…nor not only… but also as… as just as… so whether… or no sooner… than

Subordinating

time	reason	contrast	condition	place
after as as long as as soon as before by the time now that once since until when whenever while	as because in order that since so that why	although even though rather than though whereas while	as long as assuming (that) even if if provided (that) till unless until whether	where wherever

Interjections

Ah!	Eek!	Ick.	Wah.
Ahem.	Eh?	Mmmm.	Wahoo!
Ahoy!	Encore!	No!	Wee!
Amen.	Eureka!	Oh.	What!
Argh.	Flop!	Oh no!	Whoa!
Ack!	Gee whiz!	Ooops.	Wow!
Alas!	Geronimo!	Ouch.	Yahoo!
Aww.	Go!	Phew.	Yay!
Bam!	Goal!	Phooey.	Yeah!
Bang!	Golly!	Pow!	Yes!
Bingo!	Gosh!	Quick!	Yikes!
Boo!	Ha!	Rats!	Yippee!
Bravo!	Hallelujah!	S.O.S!	Yo!
Brr!	Hi!	Shhh!	Yoo-hoo!
Cheerio!	Hey!	Shoo!	Yuck.
Cheers!	Hmm.	Shucks.	Yum!
Congratulations!	Ho, ho, ho.	Thanks.	Zap!
Crash!	Hooray!	Tut-tut.	
Darn!	Howdy!	Ugh!	
Doh!	Huh?	Uh-oh.	
Duh.	Hurrah!	Umm.	

Now that you have an overview of the parts of speech, here are some clues to help you identify specific parts of speech. First, ask yourself the following yes/no questions and then refer to the basic syntax rules listed on the following page.

Parts of Speech Clues

Adjective	Can it go in front of just a noun?
Noun	Can it stand alone with "the?" (Except for most proper nouns)
Pronoun	Does it replace a noun?
Verb	Can it form a simple sentence with just a subject?
Adverb	Does it describe a verb (or adjective or adverb)?
Preposition	Can it stand alone with a noun/noun phrase to show location, time, or purpose?
Conjunction	Does it connect- words, phrases, clauses?
Interjection	Does it show emotion when used alone?

After answering "yes" to any of the above questions, check the specific word in context to see if it fits with any of the basic syntax rules. Although there are *many* syntax rules that govern the order of words in the English language, the rules on the following page provide some basic guidelines for both teachers and students.

Basic Syntax Rules

1.	Subject + verb. noun pronoun	He walks.
2.	adjective + noun	The red ball
3.	noun + linking verb + adjective (or pronoun) (linking verb= am, is, are, etc.)	The ball is red.
4.	noun ⟺ pronoun	(Pronoun replaces noun after noun is introduced.)
5.	preposition + noun (= prepositional phrase)	under the bridge
6.	**OR** adverb + verb + adverb	quietly reads **or** reads quietly
7.	Clause + conjunction + clause. (subject + verb) (subject + verb)	The students must stay inside because it is raining.
8.	Conjunction + clause, clause. (subject + verb) (subject + verb)	Because it is raining, the students must stay inside.
9.	verb + noun (transitive verb) (direct object)	Throw the ball.
10.	noun + linking verb + noun (or pronoun) (to be verbs, to seem, etc.) (noun phrase)	Whales are mammals.
11.	Noun + linking verb + prepositional phrase. (or pronoun) (to be verbs, to seem, etc.)	Squirrels were in the tree.
12.	_____ + coordinating conjunction + _____ (Can join **nouns, pronouns, verbs, prepositions, adjectives, adverbs**)	chocolate or vanilla

CPSIA information can be obtained at www.ICGtesting.com
Printed in the USA
LVOW022044081211

258519LV00003B/2/P